Other Books Available

Sports Genius Do You Know Your Sport Volume 2
History Genius Do You Know Your History Volume 1
History Genius Do You Know Your History Volume 2

© 2016 d.winning
cobberspublish@gmail.com

"The more difficult the victory, the greater the happiness in winning."
Pele

Sports Genius Do You Know Your Sport?

Volume 1

cobberspublish

Major Sports Covered

Air Aerobatic Teams	Horse Racing
American Major League Baseball	Ice Hockey
American Major League Basketball	Lawn Bowls
American Major League Football	MotoGP
Association Football	Netball
Athletics	Olympic Games
Aussie Rules Football	Polo
Archery	Rugby league
Basketball	Rugby Union
Baseball	Sailing
Boxing	Snooker
Cricket	Snowboarding
Cycling	Speedway
Fencing	Softball
Field Hockey	Squash
Formula One Motor Sport	Surfing
Golf	Tennis
Gymnastics	Waterpolo

Questions

1. In which year was the first cricket test match played between England and Australia ?

2. In which year was the New South Wales Rugby Football League formed as a professional organisation ?

3. Which horse, in 1932, won both the Australian (AJC) Derby and the Melbourne Cup ?

4. Which country appeared in 23 consecutive finals of the Davis Cup tennis tournament between 1946 and 1968 ?

5. Who was the Hawaiian credited with spreading the sport of surfing and was known as the "Father of Surfing" ?

6. Who did Muhammad Ali first fight in 1970 after he was permitted to fight again after having had his boxing license cancelled in 1967 ?

7. Which country won the men's World (field) Hockey Cup 4 times between 1971 and 2014 ?

8. In which city were the 1936 Summer Olympic Games held ?

9. Which Australian Football League (Victorian Football League) team were premiers in 1954 ?

10. In which year were the rules of association football, or soccer, first codified ?

11. Dr James Naismith is associated with which sport?

12. Which organisation was founded by Pierre de Coubertin in 1894 ?

13.   What is a "peloton" ?

14.   What sporting feat did Giuseppie Farina achieve in 1950 ?

15.   In which year were the Empire Games (Commonwealth Games) first held ?

16.   In which city in 1973 were the first FINA World Swimming Championships held ?

17.   In which year was the inaugural Sydney to Hobart yacht race ?

18.   In which country were the inaugural Winter Olympic Games held ?

19.   Which country did New Zealand defeat to win the 1987 rugby union World Cup ?

20.   Who was the Australian bowler who bowled the last English batsman, Ted Peate, to win the cricket test match played between the two countries in England in 1882?

21.   In which year was the first match of rugby league played in Brisbane ?

22.   Which horse won the first AJC Randwick (Australian) Derby in 1861?

23.   What are the four "Grand Slam" tennis tournaments?

24.   In which year was the Association of Professional Surfing first launched?

25.   In which year was the Association Football (FA) Cup competition first contested?

26. Who won the 2011 British Open golf championship?

27. In which country were the first ever world rowing championships held?

28. How many players are there on a netball team?

29. In which year was the Victorian Football Association (Australian football) formed?

30. Major League Baseball in North America is divided into which two leagues?

31. In which year was the National Basketball Association of North America formed?

32. In which sport was Walter Lindrum a world champion in 1933 and 1934 ?

33. As of the 2015 season, how many clubs made up the National Football League in the U.S.?

34. What is the name of the trophy awarded to the National Hockey League champions in North America?

35. Which sport is associated with the Webb Ellis Cup?

36. At which Olympic Games did Johnny Weissmuller, the future Hollywood star who played "Tarzan", first win 3 gold medals for swimming and one bronze medal for water polo?

37. Where were the 1968 Winter Olympic Games held?

38. What are the four major championships of men's golf?

39. What sporting feat did Gertrude Ederle of the United States achieve in 1926?

40. Who was the English cricket captain who was presented with an urn containing the"Ashes" by a group of women while he was on the English tour of Australia in 1882-83?

41. When did the Northern Rugby Football Union in England break from the Rugby Football Union to form its own competition?

42. How many times did jockey Thomas Hales ride the winner the AJC Australian Derby?

43. At which venue is the French Open tennis tournament held?

44. Who was the Association of Surfing Professionals World Tour champion in 2011?

45. What sporting event was created by Charles William Alcock?

46. Who was the Australian athlete who won the silver medal for the men's 200 metres track event at the 1968 Mexico Olympic Games? He was seen to support the American gold medallist (Tommie Smith) and bronze medallist (John Carlos) in their protest for human rights while they stood on the podium receiving their medals?

47. What was the real christen name of American baseball player, Babe Ruth?

48. The motor race that became known as the "Bathurst 1000" at a later date, was first run at which venue?

49. In which year was the Melbourne Football Club (AFL/VFL) formed?

50. In which year was the Australian professional foot race known as the Stawell Easter Gift, first run?

51. Who was the first Australian to swim the English Channel?

52. In which events did U.S. athlete Carl Lewis win four track and field gold medals at the 1984 Los Angeles Olympic Games?

53. Who was the woman golfer won the Australian Women's Open in 2000, 2002, 2008 and 2009?

54. What event did surf life saving athlete Caine Eckstein win in 2005, 2008, 2009, 2010, and 2011?

55. What are the six nations involved in rugby union's Six Nations Championship?

56. Who was the male athlete who won the 1982 and 1986 Commonwealth Games marathon?

57. Who was the first batsman in cricket to make one hundred first class centuries?

58. What was the name of the Australian yacht that unsuccessfully challenged the American yacht "Intrepid" for the America's Cup in 1967?

59. What are three sliding sports at the Winter Olympic Games?

60. At which venue did Australia defeat the English in the third cricket test of 1902?

61. What sport is associated with the annual "Tom Brock Lecture"?

62. The Australian AJC Derby is run over what distance?

63. In which year were the Australian Tennis Championships (the Australian Open), first held?

64. Up to and including January 2015, how many times was surfer Kelly Slater ASP World Tour champion?

65. Who was the boxer who won the 1964 Olympic gold medal for boxing in the heavyweight division?

66. Where, in 1888, was the world's first league of association football clubs founded ?

67. In which year was the first U.S.Open golf tournament played?

68. Who was the American athlete who won the 400 metre hurdles event at both the 1976 Montreal Olympics and at the 1984 Los Angeles Olympics?

69. What were the eight foundation clubs of the Victorian Football League, formed in 1896 ? (Aussie Rules)

70. What were the three events in which Debbie Meyer of the U.S. won gold medals during the swimming program of the 1968 Mexico Olympic Games?

71. What was the name of the national baseball competition that started in Australia in 1934?

72. Which Olympic Games were the first to have live television coverage?

73. What do the following Australian Olympic athletes have in common: Dean Capobianco, Steve Brimacombe, Andrew McManus and Joshua Ross?

74. In which year was the "Avon Decent", a Western Australian river race, first held?

75. Which nations contest the "Rugby Championship"?

76. The Australian men's Olympic association football team are known by what nickname?

77. With which sport is Australian international athlete Bill (William) Roycroft associated?

78. Who won sixteen consecutive women's British Open squash titles between 1962 and 1977?

79. Who was the world MotoGP champion between 1994 and 1998?

80. Who was the Australian cricketer who became the first player to score a century on the first morning of a test match?

81. In which year was the first "Kangaroos" (rugby league) tour of England and Wales?

82. Who was the jockey who rode Octagonal to victory in the 1996 Australian AJC Derby in a time of 2:28:41?

83. In which year was the U.S National Championship for men's singles tennis first held?

84. Who was the Association of Surfing Professionals women's champion from 2007 until 2010?

85. What colour and design jersey does the "King of the Mountain" wear in the Tour de France cycle race?

86. When and where was the Federation of Internationale de Football Association (FIFA) formed?

87. Who was the Formula One racing driver who was killed in an accident at the San Marino Grand Prix in 1994?

88. What is the name of the sport in which competitors slide a large rounded stone on ice toward a target area?

89. Which team won the first VFL/AFL premiership in 1897?

90. When did Australia first compete at a Winter Olympic Games?

91. Who was the first golfer to win the U.S Open?

92. At which Olympic Games was the women's marathon held for the first time?

93. What sport is associated with a "Salchow jump"?

94. Who was the athlete at the 1968 Mexico Olympics who won the high jump gold medal using a new type of jumping technique?

95. Super Rugby includes teams from which three nations?

96. In which three events did Australia win gold medals at the 1932 Los Angeles Olympic Games?

97. Irina Rodnina and Alexander Zaitzev are associated with which sport?

98. Who was the runner who defeated Australian and world record holder Ron Clark in the 10,000 metres at the Tokyo Olympics in 1964? Clark was placed third behind Tunisian Mohammad Gammoudi who took the silver.

99. Who was the first man to break the 15 minute barrier for the 1,500 metres in the pool?

100. England won the cricket Ashes against Australia in a triangular tournament in 1912. What was the third country involved in that tournament?

101. Who was the captain of the "Kangaroos" (rugby league) for their 1st and 2nd test matches of the first tour of England and Wales in 1908?

102. Which horse won the AJC Australian Derby in 1986, a horse ridden by Gary Stewart and trained by Frank Richie?

103. What is the name of the tennis club that holds the Wimbledon Grand Slam tennis tournament?

104. Who was the Association of Surfing Professionals women's champion from 1998 until 2003 and then again in 2006?

105. Up to the 2016 World Cup, which national team is the only team to have played in all association football World Cup tournaments?

106. Who was the Australian rower at the Amsterdam Olympics of

1928 who stopped during a round of the single sculls to allow a duck and ducklings to pass, then carried on to win the race and later the gold medal?

107. Who was the swimmer who won the Manhattan Island marathon swim five times, breaking the record in 1995 for the 48 km distance?

108. Which country won the 2015 cricket World Cup?

109. In which year did Geelong (AFL/VFL) win their first premiership?

110. Which is the only Summer Olympic Games up to London in 2012, where Australia has failed to win any medals?

111. Who is the former Australian test cricketer who has a test batting average of 102.5?

112. In which Olympic event did Sebastian Coe win consecutive gold medals?

113. Where was former AFL and West Coast Eagles footballer Don Pyke born?

114. Who was the first native-born American golfer to win the U.S. Open?

115. In which year did France play its first international rugby match against England?

116. At which Olympic Games were doping tests first introduced?

117. Former VFL /AFL player Brent Crosswell played with which three AFL/VFL/ clubs?

118. At which Olympic Games was the first Olympic torch relay performed?

119. What feat did AFL/VFL and Collingwood player Keith Bromage achieve in 1953?

120. Who was the Australian test cricketer known as the "Big Ship"?

121. Who was captain of the "Kangaroos" rugby league team for the 3rd test of their 1st tour of England and Wales?

122. In which year did Tulloch win the Australian AJC Derby?

123. Which two Grand Slam tennis tournaments are held on hard courts?

124. Mark Richards of Australia won the International Professional Surfers Championship on four occasions. What were the years in which he achieved those wins?

125. Who will host the association football World Cup in 2018?

126. Who was the former Western Australian player who kicked nine goals in his VFL/ AFL debut match in 1984?

127. What feat did Australian Joe Quinn achieve in baseball in 1884?

128. Which NFL team, established in 1933, play their home games at Heinz Field in the state of Pennsylvania?

129. In which year did Carlton (VFL/AFL) win their first premiership?

130. Which English association football club has the motto, "Nil satis nisi optimum (Only the best is good enough)?

131. Who did Jimmy Ellis fight and lose to for the vacant heavyweight title in 1970, a title which had been vacated by Muhammad Ali?

132. Up of 2015, who was the former Adelaide player who kicked thirteen goals in a match (AFL) on two occasions?

133. In which sport did Takeichi Nishi of Japan win a gold medal at the 1932 Los Angeles Olympic Games?

134. Who was the first Australian track athlete to break 10.00 seconds for the 100 metres sprint?

135. In which year was Rugby Sevens first introduced into the Commonwealth Games ?

136. Who was the Western Australian AFL/VFL footballer who was also a Rhodes Scholar?

137. Who was the Australian who won golf's U.S. Open in 2006?

138. Who was the Olympic gold medallist for the 800 metres at the Moscow Olympic Games in 1980?

139. Who was the Western Australian footballer who captained Collingwood in the VFL/AFL in 1964 and part of 1965?

140. Which Victorian Football League team did Australian test cricketer Warwick Armstrong play with?

141. In which year was the first British rugby league tour of the southern hemisphere?

142. Which horse won the 1906 Australian AJC Derby?

143. Which tennis Grand Slam tournament is played fourth in the chronological order of the series?

144. Which country was Wendy Botha representing when she won the Association of Surfing Professionals World Tour Championship in 1987-88?

145. Which two teams played the first international association football match?

146. Who was the swimmer who swam from Mexico to Cuba in 1998, a distance of 197 km, setting a new world record in the process?

147. What feat did Kyoko Iwasaki of Japan achieve at the Barcelona Olympics in 1992?

148. Who was the first man to run under 10 seconds for the 100 metres?

149. In which year did Collingwood (AFL/VFL) win their first premiership?

150. Up to and including January 2015, Kenenisa Bekele is a world record holder in which two events?

151. Where was former VFL/AFL and Carlton club champion player Alex Jesaulenko born?

152. Where were the 1972 Winter Olympics Games held?

153. Who was the Australian high jumper who was the first Commonwealth athlete to clear 7 feet in the high jump, played for Carlton in the VFL/AFL and was also the first Australian to play NFL. He was later murdered in the U.S. in 1993.

154. Who was the first Australian to captain a professional sports team in the U.S.?

155. What is the name of the trophy awarded annually to the winner of the "Six Nations" rugby union match played between England and Scotland ?

156. Who was the first indigenous player to kick 100 goals in an AFL season ?

157. Who was the sportsman who was known as "The Sultan of Swat"?

158. What feat was achieved by Australian association footballer Joe Marston in 1954?

159. Which golf tournament is sometimes referred to as "the fifth major" ?

160. Who did cricketer Don Bradman replace in the New South Wales team when he made his first class debut at the age of 19 ?

161. Which club, in 1908, became the first rugby league club to be formed in New South Wales ?

162. In which two consecutive years did jockey Darren Beadman win the AJC Australian Derby, first riding Headturner and then Fiumicino ?

163.   Which is the only Grand Slam tennis tournament played on clay?

164.   Which country is woman professional surfer, Sofia Mulanovich, originally from ?

165.   Who won the association football gold medal at the 1908 London and 1912 Stockholm Olympic Games?

166.   Who was the Australian who won the world snooker championship in 2010?

167.   Andrew Hoy is an Australian Olympian who has won gold medals at the 2000, 1996 and 1992 Olympics. In which sport was he competing?

168.   In golf, what do you call a hole in one on a par four?

169.   Who was the boxer who won the gold medal at the 1976 Montreal Olympic Games while competing in the light heavyweight division?

170.   In which year did Melbourne (AFL/VFL) win their first premiership?

171.   How many "holes in one" did Jack Nicklaus play in his career?

172.   Keith Slater played one cricket test for Australia in 1959 taking 2 wickets for 101, (2-40 and 0-61) and making one run. Which team was this against?

173.   Which Major League Baseball team did Australian Craig Shipley first play with in 1986?

174. In how many test matches did cricketer Adam Gilchrist captain Australia between 2000/2001 and 2004/2005?

175. How many rugby union caps did George Gregan gain for Australia from 1994-2007?

176. What do the following Australian sports men and women have in common: Raelene Boyle, Rick Charlesworth, Bill Roycroft, Andrew Gaze, Andrew Hoy, Dennis Green and Mervyn Wood?

177. What outstanding feat did athlete Charles Dumas of the United States accomplish in 1956?

178. How many consecutive games did Jim Stynes play for AFL club Melbourne?

179. Who was the South African golfer who won the 1965 U.S. Open ?

180. What were Don Bradman's first and second innings scores during his test debut against England in Brisbane during the 1928-29 season?

181. Which rugby league team in New South Wales, between 1908 and 1972, was known as the "Bluebags"?

182. Which horse won the Metropolitan Handicap at Sydney's Royal Randwick in 1978?

183. When did the Australian Tennis Open become known as the Australian Open, having been previously known as the Australasian Championships and the Australian Championships?

184.   Who was the woman surfer who won the Association of
       Surfing Professionals women's World Tour Championship
       in 1994, 1995, 1996 and 1997?

185.   Why was Uruguay chosen to host the first association football
       World Cup in 1930?

186.   What feat did Norma Enriqueta Basilio de Sotelo achieve in
       1968?

187.   How many players at one time can there be on the field of an
       American football game?

188.   Which English Premier League club play at Craven Cottage?

189.   Who is the only man to have captained England in both cricket
       and association football?

190.   In which year did South Melbourne/Sydney Swans, win their
       first premiership?

191.   What do the following Australian athletes have in common:
       Matthew Mitcham, Chantelle Newbery and Richard "Dick"
       Eve?

192.   Who was the U.S. woman athlete who won two gold medals and
       a silver medal at the 1932 Los Angeles Olympics, and also won
       the U.S. women's golf Open in 1948, 1950 and 1954?

193.   Who was the Perth Glory A- League player who won the
       Johnny Warren Medal in 2005/2006?

194.   In which year did Australian Mark Webber make his Formula
       One racing debut?

195. How many times was rugby union player Jonny Wilkinson capped for England between 1998 and 2011?

196. What sport is associated with the Barry Sheene Medal?

197. Who did the West Coast Eagles play in an AFL preliminary final at the WACA ground on the 24th September 1994?

198. In which year did Australian Jack Brabham win his first Formula One driver's championship?

199. For which club did Australian association footballer Craig Johnston make his English League debut in February 1978 playing against Birmingham City?

200. How many times was Australian test cricketer Don Bradman run out during his test career?

201. How many clubs made up the foundation New South Wales Rugby League competition in 1908?

202. Which premier Group One staying race, ran over 2,400 metres for three year old fillies at Randwick during the Sydney Autumn Carnival, was once known as the Adrian Knox Stakes?

203. When did the French Tennis Championships become open to all international amateurs?

204. Who became surfing's first millionaire surfer in 1989?

205. How many nations took part in the first association football World Cup in 1930?

206. Who was the Australian swimmer who won the gold medal for the 1,500 metres at the 1924 Paris Olympic Games, broke five world records and also won three silver and a bronze medal during his Olympic career?

207. Who was the first Australian golfer to win the U.S. Open?

208. Who was the first man to run the 1,500 metres in under 3 minutes 30 seconds?

209. Who was the skipper of the America's Cup defending yacht, Kookaburra III that lost to the Americans in Fremantle in 1987?

210. In which year did Richmond win their first (AFL/VFL) premiership?

211. Who was the Australian athlete who won the men's 800 metres track gold medal at the 1968 Mexico Olympic Games?

212. At which Olympics was basketball first introduced as an event?

213. In which sport did Australians Holly Crawford, Nathan Johnstone and Alex Pullin all win gold medals at the world championships in 2011?

214. How many times did Simon Lessing of Great Britain win the World Triathlon Championships?

215. Who was the Australian rugby union player who scored 29 tries for Australia between 1993 and 2004?

216. Up to and including 2015, Emma Snowsill had won the world championship in which sport, three times?

217. Who did Muhammad Ali lose his world heavyweight title to in Las Vegas on February 15th 1978?

218. Australian Troy Bayliss has been a world champion in which sport?

219. Who was the batsman who scored 325 for South Australia against Western Australia in a Sheffield Shield match at the WACA ground during the 1970/71 season?

220. What was cricketer Don Bradman's first multiple century score in a Sheffield Shield match?

221. Which New South Wales rugby league club won the premiership in the first two years of the competition?

222. Which Group One race, once known as the AJC Plate between 1873 and 1954, has been won by horses such as Grand Armee (2004 and 2005), Tulloch (1958, 1960, and 1961), Russia (1947 and 1948) and Carbine (1891,1892 and 1889)?

223. In which year did the French Tennis Championships become open so that both amateurs and professionals could compete?

224. Which surfing company was founded by Australians Allan Green and John Law in Victoria in 1969?

225. In which year did Hawthorn win their first (AFL/VFL) premiership?

226. Who did Uruguay defeat 4-2 to win the first association football World Cup in 1930?

227. Who were the four batsmen who scored centuries in the second test match of the England verses Australia Ashes series of 1970/71, a match which was played at the WACA ground in Perth which, at the time, was a first time test venue?

228. In which suburb of London is the Lord's cricket ground located?

229. Who did boxer Joe Frazier fight and defeat in defence of his world heavyweight title at Madison Square Garden in 1971, an event termed "The Fight of the Century"?

230. Who was the golfer who won the U.S. Open in 1962, 1967, 1972 and 1980?

231. On which famous Australian ground was a cricket test played for the first time on the 17th of February 1882?

232. Who was the Australian swimmer who, in Rome in 1960, won a gold medal in the 1,500m freestyle and two bronze medals, one in the 400m freestyle and the other in the 4x200m freestyle relay?

233. Who won the men's track 100 metre final at the Barcelona Olympic Games in 1992?

234. In the 1970 VFL/AFL Grand Final, Carlton player and "19th man" Ted Hopkins helped Carlton win the game when he kicked four goals in the second half. Who was the player Hopkins replaced at half time?

235. Who was the Australian vice captain when Australia won the rugby union World Cup in 1991?

236. What is the nickname of the Australian women's rugby league team?

237. Which sport had its rules developed by Scotsman, William Wilson in the late 19th century?

238. Who was the AFL player who played a record 226 games as his club's captain?

239. Who was the AFL footballer of the 1970s and 80s who had the nickname of "The Flying Door Mat"?

240. When and where did cricketer Don Bradman score his first test century?

241. In which year did Balmain win their first premiership in the New South Wales Rugby League competition?

242. At which venue is the Australasian Oakes, a race for three year old fillies over 2000m, run?

243. At which venue is the United States tennis Open held?

244. Who was the first Australian to win a major surfing title, achieving the feat in Hawaii in 1963?

245. Who won the association football World Cup which was held in Brazil in 1950?

246. In which year did St Kilda win their first (AFL/VFL) premiership?

247. Up to March 2016, how many times had Premier League club Arsenal won the FA Cup?

248. Who was the first woman outside eastern Europe to win the all-round Olympic gymnastic title?

249.   What is the second highest division in English association
        football after the Premier League?

250.   How many times did association footballer Billy Wright
        captain England?

251.   In which events did American athlete Jesse Owens win his
        four gold medals at the 1936 Berlin Olympic Games?

252.   Vic Cumberland, Magarey Medallist in 1911 and former Sturt,
        St Kilda and Melbourne footballer, was also known for
        what other accomplishment?

253.   Who was the first player in association football to score
        100 Premier League goals?

254.   Who was the Scotsman who won golf's U.S. Open
        in 1901, 1903, 1904 and 1905?

255.   How old was Australian rugby union player Mark Ella when
        he retired in 1984?

256.   Who was the AFL player who played for the following clubs:
        St Kilda, Fremantle, Essendon, Fitzroy and West Coast Eagles?

257.   Up to and including 2014,which five players had won the
        Clive Churchill Medal from the Manly-Warringah rugby
        league club?

258.   Who is the player who has scored a hat trick of goals in: the
        Premier League, Championship League One, League Two,
        the League Cup, FA Cup and for his national side?

259. Who was the boxer who defeated Muhammad Ali in March 1973, breaking Ali's jaw during the bout?

260. How many runs did Don Bradman score in the second innings of his first test in England?

261. In which year did North Sydney win their first premiership in the New South Wales Rugby League competition?

262. Which Western Australian trained horse won the Group One Australian Cup in 2001 and 2003?

263. What food is traditionally eaten at the Wimbledon tennis Open in June of each year?

264. How many times did Australian surfer Nat Young win the Bell's Beach Surfing Classic?

265. Where and when was the first women's association football World Cup?

266. In which year did North Melbourne win their first (AFL/VFL) premiership?

267. Who became coach of the Chennai Super Kings in cricket's Indian Premier League in 2008?

268. How many times did VFL/AFL and Fitzroy player Kevin Murray win his club's fairest and best award?

269. Who was the Australian who coached the Deccan Chargers in the 4th season of the Indian Premier League?

270. Who was the Australian athlete who won gold medals for the men's swimming in the 100 metre and 200 metres freestyle at the Mexico City Olympic Games in 1968 ?

271. Who coached the Wests Tigers in the NRL in 2001-2002?

272. Who was the jockey who rode Makybe Diva to Melbourne Cup wins in 2003, 2004 and 2005?

273. Who was the U.S. baseballer who played first baseman and outfielder for the New York Yankees between 1951 and 1968, appeared in 12 World Series scoring 18 home runs, played 20 All Star games and made 536 home runs during his career?

274. Who was Sammy Wanjiru?

275. How many tries did rugby union player David Campese score for Australia in test matches?

276. Which Australian cricket opening batting pair were labelled "The Kamikaze Kids" because of their frequent run outs of each other during test matches?

277. Who are two South African golfers who have won the U.S. Open twice?

278. Who was the athlete who won the gold medal for the super heavyweight division in weight lifting at the Los Angeles Olympic Games in 1984?

279. Who were the two Australians who teamed up to win the World Cup of Golf in 1989?

280. In which season did the West Indian cricket side first visit Australia?

281. In which year did Western Suburbs win their first premiership in the New South Wales Rugby League competition?

282. Which racehorse won consecutive Australian Cups accomplishing the feat in 1989 and 1990?

283. In which year was the All England Lawn Tennis and Croquet Club, originally the All English Croquet Club, founded?

284. Who were the two surfers who, in 1975, devised a rating and scoring system for surfing events?

285. What link does Silvio Gazzaniga have with association football?

286. In which year did the West Coast Eagles win their first AFL premiership?

287. Which NBA club did Red Auerbach coach to 9 titles between 1959 and 1966?

288. What is the name of the award given by the AFL Players Association for the Most Valuable Player in an AFL season?

289. Who was the Australian basketball player who was number one draft pick overall in the NBA draft of 2005?

290. Where were the 1976 Winter Olympic Games held?

291. Up to and including 2015, how many times had the U.S won the World Cup of Golf?

292. Who is the Scotsman who has won seven World Championships in snooker (as of 2015) and was the youngest player to win a world championship at 21 years old? He was snooker's number one for eight consecutive years between 1990 and 1998 and up to 2011 was runner up twice to the world title.

293. Which AFL club awards the Keith "Bluey" Truscott Medal to the club's fairest and best player of the season?

294. Eden Gardens is the home of which Indian Premier League team?

295. Up to October 2015, who was the international rugby union player who had scored the most test tries?

296. How many state games did Perth, East Perth (WAFL) and North Melbourne (VFL/AFL) player Barry Cable play?

297. Up to 2013, who are the only Australians to have played in a Major League Baseball All Star game?

298. Who, in 1987, won the last Australian Open titles in the men's and women's singles tennis tournaments played at Kooyong?

299. Up to and including 2015, how many Scotsman had won golf's U.S. Open?

300. Don Bradman was bowled for a duck in the second test in Melbourne during the "Bodyline" series of 1932-33. Who was the English bowler responsible for his dismissal?

301. Which rugby league team won consecutive New South Wales Rugby League premierships in the years 1911, 1912 and 1913?

302. At which racecourse is the Australia Cup run?

303. With which sport is Major Walter Clopton Wingfield associated?

304. How many times has American surfer Tom Curren been world champion?

305. Up to 2016, how many times had Italy won the association football World Cup?

306. In which year did Adelaide win their first AFL premiership?

307. Who was the Australian who won the gold medal for the men's 200 metre butterfly event at the 1984 Los Angeles Olympic Games?

308. Which team won cricket's "Big Bash" in 2016?

309. Up to 2015, how many times had racing car driver Mark Skaife been winner of the Bathurst 1000?

310. Zersenay Tadese, record holder for the 20km road race and the "half marathon", is from which country?

311. Who was the American baseballer nicknamed "The Yankee Clipper"?

312. Who was the Australian jockey nicknamed "The Professor"?

313. Australian cricketer Adam Gilchrist played first class cricket with which two Australian states?

314. What is the name of the "sudden death" overtime system used in rugby league football to resolve drawn matches?

315. Who was voted player of the tournament at the 1991 rugby union World Cup?

316. Who coached the Parramatta Eels rugby league team from 1997 to 2006?

317. Who was the first player to score a hat trick of goals in a match in the English Premier League of association football?

318. What was the name of the Commonwealth Games mascot in Brisbane in 1982?

319. Where is the U.S. Masters golf tournament held every year?

320. Who was the batsman who partnered Don Bradman in a stand of 451 during the 5th test at the Oval in London in 1934?

321. In which year did Canterbury-Bankstown win their first New South Wales Rugby League premiership?

322. Which horse's record for the Australia Cup was broken by Makybe Diva in 2005?

323. Who won three consecutive men's singles Wimbledon Championships between 1934 and 1936?

324. What is world champion surfer Mick Fanning's nickname?

325. Up to the 2016, how many times had Brazil won association football's World Cup?

326. Who won the AFL premiership in 2001, 2002 and 2003?

327. In cricketing terms, what is a "Nelson"?

328. Who was the Australian athlete who won the women's 100 metres butterfly gold medal at the Mexico Olympics in 1968?

329. What were the names of the two mascots at the 2012 London Olympic Games?

330. Which sport is associated with the following: a mashie, a cleek, a niblik, a brassie and a jigger?

331. Who are the only father and son pair to have won the world Formula One driver's championship?

332. Who was captain and coach of East Perth in the Western Australian Football League in 1967 and 1968?

333. Which two clubs in England did Australian association footballer John Aloisi play with?

334. In which year was the Australian Institute of Sport established?

335. The Bletisloe Cup is a trophy awarded to the winner of rugby union matches between which two countries?

336. In which sport did Australian athlete Kerry Saxby-Junna represent Australia?

337. Up to 2015, who are the two players who have
      kicked 150 goals in a VFL/AFL season?

338. In which year were the first Winter Paralympic Games held?

339. Who is the Australian woman who, among many other
      paralympic accomplishments, has won the Boston Marathon
      four times; 1997, 1998, 1999 and 2001?

340. Who captained the English cricket side during the Ashes series
      of 1936-37?

341. Which New South Wales rugby league team was runner-up
      four times to St George between St George's record
      premiership years from 1956 to 1966?

342. The Group One Blue Diamond Stakes ran at Caulfield in
      Melbourne is over what distance and for what age of horse?

343. In which year did the Davis Cup tennis tournament begin?

344. Who won the Association of Surfing Professionals World Tour
      Championship in 1999?

345. Who defeated Joe Frazier to take the heavyweight boxing title
      in a fight in Kingston Jamaica on January 22nd 1973?

346. In which year did Port Adelaide win their first AFL
      premiership?

347. Up to 2016, how many times had Germany
      (including West Germany) won the association
      football World Cup?

348. Who was the first non American player to win the U.S. Masters golf tournament?

349. Which five races represent the "The World Marathon Majors"?

350. Who was the first female jockey to win the Perth Cup?

351. Who was the Western Australian cricketer who scored 303 not out against New South Wales in a Sheffield Shield match in February 2012?

352. Who was the Australian athlete who won the women's 80 metre hurdles gold medal at the 1968 Mexico Olympic Games?

353. What common feat did the following Australians achieve in their sport: Albert Trott, Sammy Woods, Billy Murdoch, Billy Midwinter and John Ferris?

354. What feat did swimmer Gerd von Dincklage Shulinburg achieve in 1956?

355. Which team won the 2007 rugby union World Cup?

356. Which sport was invented by William George Morgan in Holyoke Massachusetts in 1895?

357. In which year were yellow tennis balls first used at Wimbledon?

358. Which National Football League team replaced the Houston Oilers in Texas which had moved to Tennessee to become the Tennessee Titans in 1997?

359. Who was the Australian who won the 1990 Berlin marathon?

360. Who made 232 for Australia against England in the 4th cricket test of 1938?

361. How many New South Wales Rugby League premierships were won by Canterbury-Bankstown during the 1980s?

362. Who was the jockey who rode four consecutive Caulfield Cup winners between 1942 and 1945?

363. Up to January 2015, how many times had Australia won the Davis Cup tennis tournament?

364. At what time of the year is the Bell's Beach Surfing Classic (Rip Curl Pro) held?

365. Up to 2016, how many times had Argentina won the association football World Cup?

366. In which year was the AFL's Essendon Football Club formed?

367. In which country is the world's "highest" golf club located?

368. With which event is Ukrainian athlete Sergey Bubka famously associated?

369. What feat did Junko Tabei of Japan accomplish in 1975?

370. What nationality were the winner and second place getter in the marathon at the 1936 Berlin Olympic Games?

371. By what other name is world famous sportsman, Edson Arantes do Nascimento, better known?

372. Up to and including 2015, who had won the most U.S Masters golf tournaments?

373. Who won the gold medal for the women's heptathlon at the 1984 Los Angeles Olympic Games?

374. What is the national sport of Bhutan?

375. What song has traditionally been sung by spectators at England's rugby union home games?

376. Which country is the birth place of the sport of taekwondo?

377. Maria de Lourdes Mutola, the 800 metres Olympic gold medallist in 2000, is from which country?

378. What was the first country to defeat England in association football at Wembley Stadium?

379. What professional sport did bank robber John Dillinger play?

380. In which year did India make its first cricket tour of Australia?

381. Which team participated in the New South Wales Rugby League competition between 1920 and 1937 with its best result being runners-up in 1926?

382. Who trained Galilee, Big Philou, Leilani, Ming Dynasty, Lets Elope and Viewed to Caulfield Cup wins?

383. Where was the first Australian Tennis Open held in 1969? (previously known as the Australian Championships)

384. Which three events make up the men's Triple Crown of Surfing?

385. Who did England defeat in the final of the 1966 association football World Cup?

386. In which year was the VFL's Fitzroy Football Club formed?

387. Which VFL club did Western Australian footballer Jack Sheedy play with in 1945?

388. What number was worn by American baseballer Babe Ruth?

389. Which English Premier League club were once called the St Domingo's F.C.

390. What is the most popular sport as a topic for a movie?

391. How many hat tricks (three goals or more in a match) did Alan Shearer score in the English Premier League?

392. What name is given to three consecutive strikes in ten pin bowling?

393. What feat was achieved by American baseballer Jack Roosevelt "Jackie" Robinson in 1947?

394. What sport are the following players famous for: Sidney Crosby, Gordie Howe and Mario Lemieux?

395. What is the emblem displayed on the shirts of England's rugby union team?

396. In which year was the first British Open golf championship played?

397.   What is the national sport of Argentina?

398.   Who was the test cricketer who was killed in a plane crash in June 2002?

399.   Where would you play a sport called biribol?

400.   What was cricketer Don Bradman's test batting average?

401.   Which New South Wales rugby league team became minor premiers in 1961, denying St George the opportunity to have 12 straight minor premierships from 1956 to 1967?

402.   How old was the thoroughbred Northerly when it won the 2002 Caulfield Cup?

403.   In which year was the Australian Open tennis moved from Kooyong to Melbourne Park?

404.   Who was the surfer who won the 2011 Billabong Pipeline Masters?

405.   Which team were runners-up to Brazil in the 1958 association football World Cup?

406.   In which year was the AFL's Collingwood Football Club formed?

407.   In which city were the 1916 Summer Olympic Games to be held but were cancelled due to World War One?

408.   What was the name of the yacht that won the first Sydney to Hobart yacht race in 1945?

409. Don White became the first national rugby union coach of which country in 1969?

410. Which association football club plays their home games at Dragon's Stadium (Estadio do Dragao)?

411. Which NFL team won the Super Bowl XLI in 2007?

412. Who defeated WBC heavyweight title holder Ken Norton to take the title on June 9th 1978?

413. English association footballer managers Arthur Johnson, Robert Firth and Michael Keeping all managed which famous European club?

414. What is the name of the game played between the champions of the UEFA Champions League and the UEFA Europa League?

415. Johnny Taylor and Otto Nothling both represented Australia in which two sports?

416. Who was the American sportsman known as "Big Aristotle"?

417. Who were the father and son who won an Olympic gold medal in the same event but 36 years apart?

418. NBA player Larry Bird played with which club between 1979 and 1992?

419. Who was the first non British golfer to win the British Open?

420. What famous feat did English cricketer Eric Hollies achieve in 1948?

421. Which two teams drew in the 1977 New South Wales Rugby League grand final?

422. Which horse won the 1932 Caulfield Cup?

423. Who was the world number one male tennis player for seven consecutive years from 1964 to 1970?

424. In which country is the Jeffreys Bay Billabong Pro surfing event held?

425. Up to 2016, how many times has the Netherlands been runners-up in the association football World Cup?

426. In which year was the AFL's Carlton Football Club formed?

427. Apart from Shaun and Geoff Marsh, which other father and son combination have played test cricket for Australia?

428. At which Australian sporting venue would you find the Victor Richardson Gates?

429. What association football club in the UK plays its home games at the Riverside Stadium?

430. Where were the 1980 Winter Olympic Games held?

431. Which NSW rugby league side went through the season undefeated in 1925?

432. What feat was achieved by Australian Jane Trumper in April 2012?

433. Against which side did association footballer David Beckham make his first appearance for the English national team?

434. Who was the first cricketer to take four wickets in four consecutive balls in international cricket?

435. In which two sports has Mike Smith represented England?

436. Who was the Brisbane Roar player who scored the penalty goal to win the 2012 A-League grand final against Perth Glory?

437. Who was the driver who took the checked flag in the controversial 2012 Formula One Bahrain Grand Prix?

438. Who is the Australian position player who has pitched in an American Major League baseball game?

439. With which AFL club did Gary Ablett Senior make his league debut in 1982?

440. Who succeeded cricketer Don Bradman as Australian test captain?

441. When did Canberra win its first New South Wales Rugby League premiership?

442. Which horse won the Melbourne Cup - Caulfield Cup double in 1997?

443. How many Grand Slam single titles did Bjorn Borg win between 1974 and 1981?

444. Who won the Billabong Pro Teahupoo surfing event in Tahiti in 2011?

445. Who is the South American player who has collected three association football World Cup medals?

446. In which year was the VFL's South Melbourne Football Club (Sydney Swans AFL) founded?

447. Who is the Australian who has won the British Open golf championship five times, the first in 1954?

448. What event did Australians Kevin Nichols, Michael Grenda, Michael Turtur and Dean Woods win gold in at the 1984 Los Angeles Olympic Games?

449. What was later discovered about 1932 Olympic women's 100 metre gold medallist Stanislawa Walasiewicz of Poland?

450. How many title defences were made by heavyweight boxer Joe Louis?

451. Who was the Balmain Tigers footballer of the 1960's known as "Golden Boots"?

452. Jack Metcafe was Australia's only medallist at the 1936 Berlin Olympics, winning a bronze medal. What was the event?

453. Australian Fabian Blattman is associated with which sport?

454. Who was captain of the Australian women's gold medal winning hockey team at the 1988 Seoul Olympic Games?

455. Up to 2015, which English premiership rugby union team has won 10 titles?

456. What was the name of the event in which Australian motor racing identity Peter Brock was killed in 2006?

457. Who won the English Premier League's Golden Boot award four times while playing for Arsenal?

458. Who was the former Australian Football League player known as "Duck"?

459. What was the name of the mascot at the 2002 Manchester Commonwealth Games?

460. Which association football club did English test cricketer Denis Compton play with?

461. Why was South Sydney awarded the 1909 premiership in the New South Wales Rugby League competition even though it didn't play a final against an opposition?

462. Which horse won the Group One Doncaster Handicap at Randwick in Sydney in 1991 and 1990?

463. Who was the world number one professional tennis player for eight years during the 1950's and early 1960's?

464. In which country is the Copa Movistar surfing event held ?

465. How many finals matches has Germany's Lothar Matthaus played in association football World Cup tournaments ?

466. In which year was the AFL's Richmond Football Club founded?

467. Who was the Australian rugby league player who coached the British side Hull to a premiership in 1991?

468. Who was the player who won two "Man of the Match" awards in the first two rugby league State of Origin games played in 1980 and 1981?

469. In which two years did Australian Greg Norman win the British Open golf championship?

470. How many title defences did world heavyweight boxing champion Larry Holmes make in his career?

471. Who was the woman track sprinter who won gold medals in the 100m, 200m and 4 x100m relay, as well as silver in the 4x 200m relay at the Seoul Olympic Games in 1988?

472. How many gold medals did Paralympian swimmer Priya Cooper win for Australia?

473. In 1964 British driver Donald Campbell set a new land speed record on Lake Eyre in Australia. What was the name of the car that he drove to set the record?

474. In which sport did Australian Michael Diamond win gold medals at Atlanta in 1996 and Sydney in 2000?

475. Which rugby union team won the English premiership in 2011?

476. Where were the first official Paralympic Games held?

477. Where was former rugby league and Balmain star Benny Elias born?

478. How many hat tricks (three or more goals in a match) did Robbie Fowler score in the English Premier League?

479. Who was cricketer Denis Lillee's first victim in test cricket?

480. Who replaced Len Hutton as English cricket captain in 1955?

481. How many premierships did New South Wales rugby league team Balmain win between 1908 and 1999?

482. Which horse won the Doncaster Handicap in 1972?

483. What is the nationality of former number one tennis player Ilie Nastase?

484. Who was the Australian surf champion known as "Rabbit"?

485. Between 1998 and 2006, how many goals had been scored by Brazil's Ronaldo in World Cup final matches?

486. In which year was the Geelong Football Club (AFL) founded?

487. NBA basketball player David Robinson played with which club between 1989 and 2003?

488. Former Australian test cricketer Brian Booth also represented Australia in which other sport?

489. How old was boxer George Foreman when he defeated Michael Moorer in 1994 to claim the World IBF and WBA heavyweight boxing titles?

490. Who was the U.S. baseballer, known as "The Iron Horse", who retired at the age of 36 and is noted for his farewell speech which he made in 1939?

491. Who were the four Australian Olympic swimmers who made up the "Quietly Confident Quartet"?

492. How old was athlete Cathy Freeman when she won a Commonwealth Games gold medal in 1990?

493. Which golfing major is known as "Glory's Last Shot"?

494. Who was the first ever Australian aboriginal Olympic gold medallist?

495. Which Australian Super Rugby side is based in Canberra?

496. Who was the former vice president of the International Olympic Committee who won a silver medal for Australia at the 1956 Melbourne Olympics in the 4 x 400 metre relay?

497. Who was the former Brisbane Broncos, Sydney Roosters, Penrith Panthers and South Queensland Crushers player who was known as "The Axe"?

498. What is the term in golf for a score of two strokes under par?

499. Which English club did former rugby league State of Origin player Michael Hancock play out his career with in 2001-2002?

500. How many test centuries did English cricketer Colin Cowdrey score in his test career?

501. Which one of the nine foundation clubs of the New South Wales Rugby League competition would only play one season?

502. The Doomben 10,000 in Brisbane is a Group One weight for age race raced over what distance since 1973?

503. How many Grand Slam singles titles were won by Australian tennis player Ken Rosewall?

504. Who was the first surfing advocate of the three finned surf board known as the "Thruster"?

505. How many goals did Archie Thompson score in an association football World Cup qualifying match for Australia against American Samoa in 2002?

506. In which year was the AFL's Western Bulldogs/Footscray founded?

507. Against which side did Australian test cricketer Matthew Hayden make his test debut in 1994?

508. In which sport did Julie Higgins win two gold medals at the 2000 Sydney Olympic Games?

509. The Frank Hyde Shield is contested between which two Sydney rugby league clubs?

510. Patrick Makau Musyoki of Kenya broke the world record for which event on September 25th 2011?

511. Which nation topped the medal tally at the 1936 Berlin Olympic Games?

512. Who was appointed coach of Melbourne Victory in the A-League in April 2012?

513. Who was the player at the centre of a racial incident that occurred during an AFL match between St Kilda and Collingwood at Victoria Park in 1993?

514. In which country are the Maccabiah Games held every four years?

515. What Super Rugby side shares the Sydney Football Stadium with both the Sydney Roosters (rugby league) and Sydney FC (association football) clubs?

516. Goldie and Isis are the reserves for which famous sporting event?

517. Name three Australians who have won the PGA championship of golf during the stroke play tournament era?

518. Who was the athlete who was disqualified for drug use after he won the 100 metre track event at the Seoul Olympic Games in 1988?

519. Which team did Chelsea defeat to win the 2012 FA Cup final?

520. Which team did English cricketer Fred Truman make his test debut against in 1952?

521. What are the two foundation clubs of the New South Wales Rugby League competition that are still playing?

522. Which winner of the Melbourne Cup and Caulfield Cup, also won the Doomben Cup in Brisbane in 1998?

523. How many Grand Slam tennis titles were won by Australian Roy Emerson?

524. Who was the first woman to win the world championship of surfing twice?

525. Who was the English player who scored three goals in the association football World Cup final against West Germany in 1966?

526. In which year was the AFL's Hawthorn Football Club founded?

527. Who is the Portuguese association football manager who is commonly known as "The Special One"?

528. Who was the St Kilda player who kicked his 500th AFL career goal in a match against Melbourne in 2012?

529. The NFL team, the Jaguars, are located in which city of the U.S.?

530. Which national side won the 2006 and 2009 World Baseball Classic?

531. Who was the Norwegian and Beijing Olympic Games silver medallist swimmer who died in 2012 aged 26?

532. In which event did U.S. athlete Mike Powell break a world record on August 30th 1991 while competing at the World Championships ?

533. How many races did racehorse Black Caviar win as a two year old?

534. Who coached the NBA's Los Angeles Lakers between 2005 and 2011?

535. Which rugby union club awards the Pilecki Medal for the best player from that club in a season?

536. Who was appointed coach of Melbourne Heart in the Australian A-league in May 2012?

537. Which English Premier League team was relegated in 2012 after 11 years in the top flight?

538. Who trained champion Australian racehorse "Northerly"?

539. Who was the first Australian golfer to win a "Major"?

540. W.G. Grace was an English test cricketer. What did the letters W. G. stand for?

541. Which team was expelled from the New South Wales Rugby League competition in 1929?

542. Which horse won the Group One Epsom Handicap at Randwick in 1932 and 1933?

543. Who was the tennis player who was runner-up to Roy Emerson 5 times in Grand Slam singles finals?

544. Who was the professional surfer who drowned while surfing at Mavericks, Half Moon Bay in Northern California in December 1994?

545. What do association footballers Franz Beckenbauer of Germany and Mario Zagallo of Brazil have in common?

546. In which year was the AFL's St Kilda Football Club established?

547. What were the two demonstration sports at the 1956 Melbourne Olympic Games?

548. Up to 2015, who is the association footballer and Barcelona player who has also been the captain of the Argentine national team since 2011?

549. In which year was the AFL's "Rising Star" award first presented?

550. At what venue on May 12th 2012, did race horse Black Caviar win its 21st consecutive race ?

551. In which Olympic Games did the U.S. basketball "Dream Team" which included players from the NBA, participate for the first time in an Olympic Games?

552. At what venue did AFL's Greater Western Sydney win their first ever AFL game in May 2012?

553. What colour jersey is worn by the over all leader of the general classification in the Giro de Italia cycle race?

554. Against which team in 2012, did Fremantle Dockers player Matthew Pavlich kicked his 500th AFL goal ?

555. Which side lost the rugby union Super 12 final to the Crusaders in 2000?

556.   A world record for the men's track 4 x 100 relay was set in
        September 2011 by four athletes from which country?

557.   How many times did Alan Shearer win the English Premier
        League's Golden Boot award?

558.   Which team did Manchester City defeat to win the English
        Premier League Championship in 2012?

559.   Up to 2015, how many times had golfer Tiger
        Woods won the PGA championship?

560.   Who was the captain of the Australian cricket test team when
        they won the Ashes in the 1899, 1901-02 and 1902 series?

561.   Which team did Balmain merge with in 1999 to form the West
        Tigers in the National Rugby League competition?

562.   Over what distance is the Epsom Handicap at Randwick in
        Sydney run?

563.   Who was the first black tennis player to be selected for the
        U.S. Davis Cup team?

564.   Who is considered to be the "father of modern surfing"?

565.   What notable feat was achieved by Italian association football
        coach Vittorio Pozzo?

566.   In which year was the AFL's North Melbourne/Kangaroos
        Football Club founded?

567.   What feat did Venezuelan Pastor Maldonado achieve in May
        2012?

568. What was the 2012 cricket series score between Australia and the West Indies?

569. How many goals did Gary Ablett Senior kick in the 1989 AFL grand final?

570. Why was Cuban, Angel Matos banned for life from international competition during the 2008 Summer Olympic Games?

571. Who were the first father and son to represent Australia in rugby league?

572. What nationality is association football manager Manuel Pellegrini?

573. Who was the Melbourne VFL/ AFL footballer who lost his life during World War Two on July 31st 1941?

574. Which Olympic Games were known as the "Austerity Games"?

575. Which Super Rugby team finished with the "Wooden Spoon" in 2006?

576. Who was the motor cycle rider who was killed in the Malaysian Grand Prix in October 2011?

577. Who was considered to be the world's highest paid athlete in 1990?

578. Who did Japan defeat to win the women's association football World Cup in 2011?

579. David Rudisha of Kenya set a world record for which event in Italy in 2010?

580. Up until March 2016, which cricketer had scored the most test runs?

581. Which team replaced Newcastle in the New South Wales Rugby League competition when Newcastle departed to join a Newcastle competition in 1909?

582. Which Group One race, first run in 1957, run at Rosehill in Sydney, run over 1,200 metres at set weights and, up to January 2012, was the world's richest race for two year olds?

583. Who was the male Czech tennis player who won 8 Grand Slam singles titles and who was ranked number one player for in 1985-87 and 1989?

584. Up to 2016, how many "Triple Crowns of Surfing" titles had Sunny Garcia won?

585. What award was given to Just Fontaine of France at the 1958 association football World Cup?

586. In which year did the West Coast Eagles play their first season in the AFL?

587. Who, in 1916, was the first player to win the PGA championship of golf (match play era)?

588. Who was the Australian jockey who served a gaol term of 7 months in Hong Kong and a further 13 months in Australia for a conspiracy tips-for-bets scam?

589. Which NBA club did Shaquille O'Neal first play with between 1992 and 1996?

590. What is the largest participant sport in the world?

591. In which year was the first Oxford-Cambridge boat race held?

592. In what type of car did Garth Tander and Nick Percat win the Bathurst 1000 in 2011?

593. Who was considered by Forbes to be the world's top earning athlete of 1996?

594. Who won the U.S Open golf in 2011, scoring 268 and becoming the youngest player to win the Open since Bobby Jones in 1923?

595. What is the fourth team that shares the AAMI stadium in Melbourne after, Melbourne Storm (rugby league), Melbourne Heart (soccer) and Melbourne Victory (soccer)?

596. Who won the Laureus World Sports award for men in 2000?

597. Which team did Chelsea defeat to win the Champions League trophy in May 2012?

598. Javier Sotomayor of Cuba set a world record in which event in Spain in July1993?

599. Who was the first AFL player to be charged with staging, after a match in May 2012?

600. How many test matches did cricketer Don Bradman play in his career?

601. Who did the North Sydney Bears merge with in 2000 only to split again in 2002 and return to the New South Wales Rugby League competition, the second tier competition of the National Rugby League?

602. Who was the jockey who rode the winner of the Golden Slipper Stakes at Rosehill for four years in a row; 1989 to 1992?

603. How many tennis Grand Slam singles titles did American John McEnroe win?

604. What feat did Australian Phyllis O'Donnell achieve in 1964?

605. Who was awarded the Golden Boot award at the association football World Cup in South Africa in 2010?

606. Which year was Adelaide Football Club's first season in the AFL?

607. Up to the end of the 2015 season,what is the name of the home ground of AFL's Greater Western Sydney?

608. Who won the 2012 Monaco Formula One Grand Prix?

609. Who did heavyweight boxing champion Larry Holmes defend his title against in June 1982?

610. How many times did South African Gary Player win the Australian Open golf tournament?

611. In 2006 AFL club St Kilda were stripped of their two premiership points which they had been awarded for a drawn match in Launceston. The umpires however, who had failed to hear the final siren, had allowed 20 extra seconds of play in

which St Kilda had scored two points to level the score. Their opponents were later declared the winner and given the four premiership points.Who were St Kilda's opponents that day?

612.   What feat did Canadian Ryder Hesjeda achieve in May 2012?

613.   Who won the 2012 Formula One Canadian Grand Prix?

614.   Who did Maria Sharapova defeat to win the 2012 French Tennis Open?

615.   Which Super Rugby side represents the Auckland, North Harbour and Northland areas in New Zealand?

616.   Which team did the Gold Coast Suns defeat in round four of 2011 to win their first ever AFL game?

617.   Who was the golfer who won the 2012 U.S. Open?

618.   Why was Argentinian tennis player David Nalbandian fined $12,500 at the final of the Queens Club tournament in June 2012?

619.   Which association football national side did Dutchman Guus Hiddink manage between 2006 and 2010?

620   What was Australian cricketer, Mark Taylor's highest test score?

621.   Which club of the New South Wales Rugby League competition competed between the years 1910 and 1920 under the nickname "The Dales"?

622. The horse race known as the Melbourne Stakes was changed to what other name after 1936?

623. How many Grand Slam singles tennis titles did American Jimmy Connors win?

624. Where is the U.S Open of Surfing held each year?

625. What is the name of the oldest association football club in the world?

626. In which year did the Brisbane Bears play their first match in the AFL?

627. Who won the British MotoGP at Silverstone in June 2012?

628. What is the name given to a golf competition where the winner is the individual or team which wins the most holes?

629. What was the name of the player who made his U.S. Open golf debut in 2012 at the age of 14?

630. Which Olympian was known as the "Flying Housewife"?

631. Who was the West Indian batsman who scored a record for a No.11 test batsman by scoring 95 against England in the 3rd test at Edgbaston in 2012?

632. Who was the Czech player, ranked 100 in the world at the time, who eliminated Rafael Nadal from the 2012 Wimbledon tennis tournament?

633. Who was the Italian striker who scored twice against Germany to put Italy into the Euro 2012 final against Spain?

634. Who was the first Australian baseball player to play in a World Series?

635. Who were runners-up to the Bulls in the Super Rugby final in 2009?

636. Who won the 2012 Dutch MotoGP?

637. What is the name of the NFL team which is located in Colorado in the U.S.?

638. What was the final score in the Euro 12 final between Spain and Italy?

639. What feat did Agnieszka Radwanska achieve when she defeated American Victoria Azarenka in the 2012 Wimbledon ladies singles tennis semi final?

640 What record score did Victoria make in a Sheffield Shield cricket match in 1926?

641. In which year did Penrith enter the New South Wales Rugby League competition?

642. What is the venue for the Group One horse race known as the Manikato Stakes?

643. How many Grand Slam women's singles tournament titles did American Chris Evert win?

644. Who won the 2016 Australian Formula One Grand Prix?

645.   In which city is the English professional association football
        club of Aston Villa located?

646.   In which year did AFL club, the Brisbane Bears, merge with
        the Fitzroy Lions to form the Brisbane Lions ?

647.   Who won the Wally Lewis Medal for the best player of the
        State of Origin series in July 2012?

648.   Who won the 2012 women's tennis singles final at
        Wimbledon?

649.   Which two traditional test grounds in England were not
        included in the Ashes test schedule of 2013?

650.   Who did Muhammad Ali fight and lose to in his final fight of
        his career?

651.   American Michael Johnson set a world record for which event
        at the World Athletic Championships in Spain in August 1999?

652.   Who won the Laureus World Sports award for men in 2012?

653.   How many times was racing driver Peter Brock a winner of the
        Bathurst 1000?

654   Who was the winner of golf's British Open in 2011?

655.   Up to and including 2015, what is the combined total of titles
        won by the Crusaders in Super 12, Super 14 and Super Rugby?

656.   Who was the last British men's singles player to reach the final
        at Wimbledon before Andy Murray achieved the feat in 2012?

657. Against which side did AFL star Buddy Franklin kick his 500th AFL goal?

658. Who was runner up to Roger Federer in the Wimbledon men's singles final in 2012?

659. Who won the British 2012 Formula One Grand Prix at Silverstone?

660. What record low score did South Australia make in an innings of a Sheffield Shield cricket match in 1955?

661. In which year did the Parramatta Eels enter the New South Wales Rugby League competition?

662. The horse race, once known as the Freeway Stakes at Moonee Valley, was changed to what other name in 1984?

663. How many Grand Slam women's singles tournament titles did Steffi Graf win?

664. What do you call a surfer who rides with his right foot forward?

665. Which English based club won the UEFA Champions League in 1982?

666. In which year did the South Melbourne Football Club move to Sydney to become the Sydney Swans?

667. Which Scottish Premier League team was relegated to the third division in 2012?

668. Who won the 2012 Tour de France cycle race?

669. Who was the driver who won the 2012 German Formula One Grand Prix?

670. How old was American athlete Bob Mathias when he won gold in the decathlon at the London Olympic Games in 1948?

671. Who became the first South African cricketer to score a triple test century?

672. Who was the Australian swimmer known as "The Missile"?

673. Who carried the Australian flag at the opening of the 2012 London Olympic Games?

674. Athlete Daniel Komen set a world record for the 3,000 metres in a time of 7:20:67 in September 1996 in Italy. What country is he from?

675. In which city are the Super Rugby team, the Highlanders, based?

676. How many medals has American swimmer Michael Phelps won in Olympic Games competition?

677. In which sport would you use an Epee?

678. Who was the golfer who won the 2012 U.S. PGA golf championship?

679. The Iditarod race is a 1,200 mile dog sled race run between which two cities?

680. Up until 2015, who had scored the most runs in

Sheffield Shield/Pura Cup cricket?

681.   In which year did the Newcastle Knights enter the New South Wales Rugby League competition?

682.   What was the name of the jockey that rode Archer to victory in the 1861 and 1862 Melbourne Cups?

683.   How many Grand Slam women's singles tournament titles did Martina Navratilova win?

684.   In which country is the Hainan Surfing Classic held?

685.   Which team won the UEFA Champions League in 1977, 1978, 1981, 1984 and 2005?

686.   In which year was the Port Adelaide Football Club established?

687.   American Julie Krone is associated with which sport?

688.   In tennis the French word "l'oeuf" means "egg". What does this symbolise?

689.   Which AFL club had its theme song adapted from the song "Good-bye Dolly Gray"?

690.   Which English sporting event has been conducted since 1829, is run over 6.8 km, begins in Putney and ends in Morelake ?

691.   Which NFL team won Super Bowl IV in 1970, defeating the MinnesotaVikings?

692.   Which two teams in rugby union compete for the Bowring Bowl?

693. What was the first communist country to win tennis' Davis Cup?

694. What sporting first did Gary Muhrcke achieve in September 1970?

695. In which city are the Super Rugby team known as the Hurricanes, based?

696. What was the name of the Italian international player who joined "A" League side Sydney FC in 2012 for a then Australian record fee?

697. Who won the women's singles final at the U.S. tennis Open in September 2012?

698. UK athlete Jonathan Edwards set a world record for which event at the World Championships in Sweden in 1995?

699. Jurgen Schult of Germany (GDR) set a world record for which event in June 1986?

700. What was Don Bradman's Sheffield Shield batting average?

701. In which year did the Brisbane Broncos enter the New South Wales Rugby League competition?

702. Which horse won the Newmarket Handicap at Flemington in 2011?

703. How many Grand Slam finals did Australian tennis player Evonne Goologong Cawley play in?

704. How old was surfer Layne Beachley when she turned professional?

705. Which team won the UEFA Champions League in 2011?

706. In which year did Port Adelaide first play in the AFL?

707. Who won the 2012 Formula One Italian Grand Prix?

708. How many times did Greg Norman win the Australian Open golf tournament?

709. Who briefly held the WBA heavyweight boxing title from October 1979 to March 1980?

710. Where did Australia finish on the medal tally at the 2012 London Paralympics?

711. Whose AFL jumper sold for $100,000 in 2012?

712. Who was the former AFL player was known as "The Dominator"?

713. Who was the Australian jockey who was banned for two years after he had threatened chief steward Terry Bailey?

714. Which horse won the Victoria Derby at Flemington in 2012?

715. Which Super Rugby team is based in Pretoria, South Africa?

716. What world boxing title did Australian fighter Danny Green win in November 2012?

717. Who won the 2012 Formula One driver's championship?

718. What is the emblem of the French national rugby union team?

719. Which horse won the Railway Stakes at Ascot racecourse in Perth in 2012?

720. What was Western Australian cricketer Geoff Marsh's highest Sheffield Shield/Pura Cup score?

721. Apart from Brisbane and Newcastle,what was the name of the third club admitted to the New South Wales Rugby League competition in 1988?

722. The Newmarket Handicap at Flemington in Melbourne is run over what distance?

723. What do the following tennis players have in common: Mats Wilander, Jimmy Connors, Andre Agassi, Rafael Nadal and Roger Federer?

724. Who was Australian surfing champion in 1972 and 1974?

725. Which Scottish team won the UEFA Champions League in 1967?

726. In which year did the Fremantle Dockers enter the AFL competition?

727. The Centenary Quaich is a rugby union trophy awarded to the winner of a match at the Six Nations tournament between which two nations?

728. Up to an including 2015, how many times had WAFL club East Fremantle been runners-up to the premiership?

729. Who was the Dutchman who won the overall standings at the 2013 Tour Down Under cycling event?

730. Which two gridiron teams contested the 47th Super Bowl in 2013?

731. What feat did American athlete Alice Coachman achieve at the 1948 London Olympic Games?

732. What famous event did racehorse Auroras Encore win in April 2013?

733. Who won the U.S. Masters golf tournament in April 2013?

734. How many times did Jack Nicklaus win the Australian Open golf tournament?

735. Which Super Rugby team is based in Bloemfontein, South Africa?

736. What was the name of the boat that took line honours in the 2012 Melbourne to Hobart yacht race?

737. At which racecourse did Black Caviar win her 25th straight race?

738. Who was the South African batsman who scored 110 not out in the 2nd cricket test against Australia in Adelaide in November 2012, denying Australia victory and hanging on to draw the match?

739. Which Western Australian horse won his eleventh race in succession by winning the Winterbottom Stakes at Ascot in November 2012?

740. How many Sheffield Shield matches did cricketer John Inverarity play?

741. What three names did the Gold Coast club use during its time in the New South Wales Rugby League, Australian Rugby League and National Rugby League, up to 1998?

742. At which racecourse is the Oakleigh Plate run over 1,100 metres?

743. Up to the end of 2015, how many Grand Slam singles titles had Swiss tennis player Roger Federer won?

744. Who won the women's Rip Curl Pro at Bell's Beach in 2011?

745. Which European club won the UEFA Champion League 9 times from 1956 to 2002?

746. In which year did the Gold Coast Suns play their first season of AFL football?

747. Who was the jockey who rode the 2012 Cox Plate winner, Ocean Park?

748. What are the names of the three NFL teams that are located in California?

749. Which team won the 2013 "Big Bash" cricket series?

750. Who was considered by Forbes to be the world's top earning athlete of 1995?

751. Who partnered Australian Casey Dellacqua in the final of the women's doubles at the 2013 Australian Open tennis tournament?

752. Who was the Brazilian woman footballer who was named best female footballer of the year in 2006, 2007, 2008, 2009 and 2010?

753. Who became the first runner to win the Stawell Easter Gift off scratch, accomplishing the feat in 1975?

754. What was the last scheduled Formula One Grand Prix of 2013?

755. Which Super Rugby team is based in Cape Town, South Africa?

756. Which horse won the Australian Oaks at Randwick in Sydney in April 2013?

757. Which team won the A-League football championship in 2013?

758. Who was the socceroo player who scored for Australia against Iraq in June 2013 to secure Australia a place in the 2014 World Cup?

759. Who were the two tennis players who contested the 2013 women's singles final at Wimbledon?

760. What was cricketer Don Bradman's highest Sheffield Shield score?

761. Which two teams were admitted to the New South Wales Rugby League competition at the beginning of the 1982 season?

762. What is the name of the Group One weight for age race, run over 1,500 metres at Rosehill in Sydney in April, first run in

1972 and was first classified as a Group One race in 2005?

763. Who won the gold medal for the men's singles tennis at the 2008 Beijing Olympic Games?

764. What are the three events of the women's surfing "Triple Crown"?

765. How old was Essendon's Dick Reynolds when he won his first AFL/VFL Brownlow Medal?

766. Which club won the UEFA Champion League title in 1979 and 1980?

767. Which horse won the 2012 Melbourne Cup?

768. Which team won the 2013 preseason AFL NAB Cup?

769. Which Gai Waterhouse horse won the 2013 Golden Slipper?

770. Who won the men's singles tennis final at the 2012 U.S. Open?

771. Who was the New Zealand athlete who was awarded a gold medal after the winner of the event was disqualified for being a drug cheat during the 2012 London Olympic Games?

772. Who was the rider who had urine thrown at him during the 2013 Tour de France?

773. Who was the golfer who won the 2013 British Open?

774. Who won the 2013 Formula One Singapore Grand Prix?

775. Which Super Rugby team is based in Johannesburg, South Africa?

776. Who knocked out John Tate to take the WBA heavyweight title in March 1980?

777. Who did Serena Williams defeat to win the 2013 U.S. Open women's singles tennis final?

778. Who did Australian cyclist Anna Meares defeat to win the women's sprint final at the 2012 London Olympic Games?

779. Who won the 2013 AFL Brownlow Medal?

780. Who was the bowler who took a record 513 Sheffield Shield wickets during his career?

781. In which year was the first rugby league State of Origin match played in Australia?

782. The Queensland Derby is a Group One race held at Eagle Farm in Brisbane. The first race in 1868 however was run in which other town?

783. Who was the tennis player who won the 2011 men's singles final at the Australian Open, U.S. Open and Wimbledon Championships?

784. Where in France in 2006, was the venue of the surfing event known as the Quicksilver Pro?

785. Which Victorian Football League team was once known as the Maroons?

786. Which English club was runners-up in the UEFA Champions League in 1975?

787. What is the name of the trophy awarded to the winner of the women's singles at the French Open tennis tournament?

788. What was the name of the Australian who skippered the winning America's Cup yacht during the 2013 series in San Francisco against New Zealand?

789. Who won the 2013 Clive Churchill Medal for the best player in the Australian Rugby League grand final?

790. Who was the AFL/VFL footballer known as "The Doc" or "Mr Magic"?

791. Who defeated Russian Alexander Povetkin to retain the WBA, IBF, WBO and IBO world heavyweight titles on Saturday 5th of October 2013?

792. Who became the youngest winner of a Moto-GP championship title when he finished third at the Valencia Moto-GP in November 2013?

793. Who won the Australian PGA golf championship in November 2013?

794. Which team did Indian cricketer Sachin Tendulkar play against in his last test match?

795. Which Super Rugby team is based in Durban, South Africa?

796. Who won the 2013 Australian Masters golf tournament?

797. Which team won cricket's 2015 "Big Bash" tournament?

798. In which suburb of Sydney is the New South Wales Golf Club located?

799. What nationality is international woman golfer Jiyai Shin?

800. How many Sheffield Shield wickets did cricketer Denis Lillee take in his career?

801. What were the names of the four foundation clubs of the Queensland Amateur Rugby Football League (Queensland Rugby League)?

802. What is the name of the Queensland Group One race, first raced in 1951, a race held in June each year, ran over 2,400 metres at Eagle Farm and is a set weight race for 3 year old fillies?

803. How old was German Boris Becker when he won the Wimbledon men's singles tennis final in 1985?

804. Who was runner-up to Joel Parkinson in the Rip Curl Pro surfing event at Bell's in 2011?

805. The rules of which sport were first written up by Tom Wills, William Hammersley, J.B. Thompson and Thomas H. Smith in May 1859?

806. Which English club was runners-up in the UEFA Champions League in 2009 and 2011?

807. Who won rugby league's Dally Messenger Medal in 2013?

808. Who was the tennis player who received the 2013 Newcombe Medal, Australia's top tennis honour?

809. Who defeated WBA heavyweight champion Mike Weaver to take the title in December 1982?

810. Who was the manager of association football club Perth Glory between 1996 and 1998?

811. Which three teams did Australia draw in the first round of the 2014 World Cup of association football?

812. What was the name of the mascot at the 2006 Melbourne Commonwealth Games?

813. Which Western Australian Football League team were once known as "The Cardinals"?

814. Who was the player who scored 4 tries for the All Blacks in the semi final against England in the 1995 World Cup in South Africa?

815. George Gregan and Stirling Mortlock have each played over 100 games for which Super Rugby club?

816. Who is the Australian golfer known as "The Dark Shark"?

817. Dennis Baker played Sheffield Shield cricket for which two states between 1972 and 1982?

818. Which two AFL clubs did former Hawthorn player Gary Ayres coach?

819. With which sport is Sam Backo associated?

820. Who was the bowler who conceded a record 4 for 362 in an innings of a Sheffield Shield cricket match?

821. In which year was the Brisbane Rugby Football League first formed?

822. Which horse won the Railway Stakes at Ascot in Perth in 2000?

823. Who was the American tennis player who won the men's singles title at Wimbledon in 2000?

824. Who was the Australian woman surfer who won the World Surf Riding Championships in 1990?

825. Which AFL club won the Victorian Football Association premiership in 1896?

826. Which two English clubs were runners-up in the UEFA Champions League in 2006 and 2008 respectively?

827. Which two cities lost out to Tokyo for the 2020 Olympic Games?

828. Who did the Dutch defeat 2-0 to win the gold medal for the women's hockey at the London Olympic Games in 2012?

829. What number rugby jersey did Nelson Mandela wear when he presented the rugby union World Cup to Springbok captain Francois Pienaar in 1995?

830. How long does the winner of the U.S. Masters golf tournament get to to keep his Green Jacket?

831. Who were the two athletes that won gold medals for Australia at the 1948 London Olympic Games?

832. Who was the player who played a record 181 games with the A-League club, Adelaide United?

833. Which horse won the 2012 Caulfield Cup?

834. Who was the cricketer who was named International Cricket Council's "Cricketer of the Year" for 2013?

835. Phil Waugh was named captain of which Super Rugby team in 2007?

836. Who was the player who scored his first test hundred for Australia in the 5th test match at the Oval in 2013?

837. Who was crowned world APS (surfing) champion for 2013?

838. The oldest permanent fixture at Lord's cricket ground is that played between which two well known schools?

839. How many test wickets did Don Bradman take?

840. Up to 2015,what are the best bowling figures for an innings in Sheffield Shield cricket?

841. What venue was home to rugby league in Brisbane up until 1932?

842. The South Australian Derby over 2,500 metres, is run at which racecourse?

843. Who won the Wimbledon men's singles tennis final in 2002?

844. What sport is also known as pugilism?

845. Which VFL (AFL) club did champion goal kickers Horrie Clover and Harry Vallance play for during the 1920's and 1930's respectively?

846. Which European club were runners-up in the UEFA Champions League five times from 1973 to 2003?

847. In which Victorian town is a bronze monument of the champion Australian mare Black Caviar located?

848. Who was the rugby league player known as "The Godfather of Manly"?

849. Who was rugby league's International Federation, "Player of the Year" for 2013?

850. The Houston Texans are one of two teams in the NFL which are based in Texas. What is the second team?

851. Which yacht took line honours in the 2013 Sydney to Hobart yacht race?

852. Who was voted by the Golf Writers Association of America as "Golfer of the Year" in 2013?

853. Who was captain of the first Hawthorn side to win a VFL/AFL premiership?

854. Who was named "Australian Cyclist of the Year" for 2013?

855. Will Genia won the award for the best player at which Super Rugby club in 2011?

856. Which horse won the "Magic Millions" on Queensland's Gold Coast in January 2014?

857. What J-league club did Shinji Ono intend on joining when he announced he was leaving A-League club Wanderers in January 2014?

858. In what position did Australian Mark Webber finish in the 2013 Australian Formula One Grand Prix?

859. Who were the driving pair who won the "Bathurst 1000" in 2012?

860. Who was the bowler who took 10 for 44 in a Sheffield Shield match in Perth in 1967?

861. Which club won the Brisbane Rugby League premiership 24 times between 1909 and 1995?

862. The Sydney Cup thoroughbred race is run over what distance?

863. What do the following tennis players have in common: Ivan Lendl, Patrick Rafter, Roger Federer, Lleyton Hewitt and Jelena Dokic?

864. In the eighteenth century, Englishman Jack Broughton made up a code of rules for which particular sport?

865. Which VFL/AFL team was once known as "The Bloods"?

866. Which English Premier League team started out as Dial Square in 1886?

867. At which Olympic Games did Roger Federer win a silver medal for the men's singles tennis event?

868. With which sport is Australian gold medalist and Olympian Jennifer Armstrong associated?

869. Which English cricket test ground has the Brian Statham End to the south and the Pavilion End to the north?

870. In which events did Australian athlete Shirley Strickland win two bronze medals at the 1948 London Olympic Games?

871. Who was the world sports star who had a fashion label known as CR7?

872. Who was the Formula One driver who replaced Mark Webber as the Red Bull partner of Sebastian Vettel in 2014?

873. Who was the "Man of the Match" in the Boxing Day cricket test at the MCG in December 2013?

874. Who was the Manchester United footballer who was involved in the 1995 "kung fu kick incident" against a Crystal Palace fan which resulted in the player's suspension.

875. Which team did the Super Rugby team Western Force defeat in 2006 to register the club's first win in the competition?

876. Which team won the 48th NFL Super Bowl in 2014?

877. Which other major horse race at Flemington is raced on the same day programme as the Victoria Derby?

878. What was the name of the 16 year old Margaret River surfer who defeated world champion surfer Kelly Slater in the ASP Rip Curl Pro in Portugal in October 2013?

879. Who was the English bowler who bowled Ashton Agar for 98 in the opening test of the Ashes series at Trent Bridge in July 2013 denying Agar of a century for Australia in his first test match?

880. Who is the wicketkeeper who has taken a record 546 dismissals in the Sheffield Shield/Pura Cup cricket competition?

881. Which club won the last Brisbane Rugby League grand final which was held in 1997?

882. Which horse won consecutive Sydney Cups in 1998 and 1999?

883. How many times did John Newcombe win the Wimbledon men's singles tennis final?

884. John Graham Chambers drafted a set of boxing rules in 1865 which became known by what name?

885. Who did Collingwood defeat in three successive VFL grand finals played in 1927, 1928 and 1929?

886. Which English team were Premier League champions in 1994-95?

887. Who was appointed as Newcastle Jets caretaker coach after the sacking of Gary Van Egmond from the A-league team in January 2014?

888. Who did the Australian tennis Davis Cup team lose 5-0 to in early February 2014?

889. Why is the Winter Olympics event, the skeleton, named as such?

890. Who was the former AFL footballer who was known as "The Kid"?

891. Which horse won the 2014 Oakleigh Plate at Caulfield?

892. Who won the 2012 MotoGP at Aragon in Spain?

893. Alex Pullin, Australia's snowboard cross world champion is also known by what nickname?

894. To which association football league does the club Vegalta Sendai belong?

895. Who was the first Victorian born player to be included in the Australian Wallabies rugby union team? He is also a notable Australian historical figure.

896. Which two teams played off in the Sochi Winter Olympics men's ice hockey final?

897. Who is Vladimir Klitschko?

898. Which horse won the Australia Cup at Flemington in March 2014?

899. Which nation won tennis' 2013 Hopman Cup final played in Perth, Western Australia?

900. Who was the wicketkeeper who contributed to 12 dismissals in a Sheffield Shield cricket match in 1938?

901. Which international team did the Australian rugby league side beat 86-6 at Gateshead in the United Kingdom at the 1995 World Cup?

902. In which year did racehorse Kingston Town win the Sydney Cup?

903. In which years did Australian Patrick Rafter win the U.S. Open singles title?

904. What set of rules preceded the Marquess of Queensbury Rules for boxing?

905. Which AFL club scored 37.17 (239) against Brisbane in 1992?

906. Which English Premier League club moved to Reebok Stadium in 1997, moving from their former home ground of Burnden Park which had been their home for 102 years?

907. What are the two conferences called that make up American football's National Football League?

908. Who won the women's Brisbane Tennis International singles title in January 2013?

909. Who won the Australian Ladies Masters golf tournament at Royal Pines on the Gold Coast in February 2013?

910. Who was the athlete who took out the Australian Iron Man title at Coolum in February 2014?

911. Who was the winner of the AFL rising star award for 2013?

912. Which team became the Australian Women's National Basketball League champions in March 2014?

913. What was the name of the mascot for the 2010 Delhi Commonwealth Games?

914. What is the hometown of Australian professional surfer Stephanie Gilmore?

915. Super Rugby team, Melbourne Rebels, played their inaugural match against which team in February 2011?

916. What is the name of the team that won the America's Cup yacht race series in 2013?

917. Which three English county sides did Australian cricketer Stuart Law play with between 1996 and 2009?

918. Who is the American sportsman who is known as "The Baltimore Bullet"?

919. Who was the winner of the men's singles tennis title at the Australian Open in 2014?

920. Which two players have each taken 189 catches in Sheffield Shield /Pura Cup cricket during their career?

921. Which national rugby team defeated Australia 38-4 at the Sydney Cricket Ground in 1952?

922. Which horse won the Sydney Cup in 1967?

923. In which year did Goran Ivanisevic win the Wimbledon men's singles tennis title?

924. Who was the last fighter to be world champion under the London Prize Ring Rules of boxing in 1882?

925. How many VFA premierships did Footscray win?

926. Which English Premier League club was bought by Russian billionaire Roman Abramovich in 2003?

927. Who was the winner of the 2014 Australian Formula One Grand Prix?

928. Where were the Winter Olympic Games held in 1984?

929. Who won the 2012 Clive Churchill Medal for the best player in the NRL Grand Final?

930. In which event did Jessica Gallagher win a bronze medal at the Sochi Winter Paralympic Games in March 2014?

931. In which Summer Olympic Games did the Soviet Union compete for the first time?

932. Which team won the Premier's Plate in the Australian A-League in March 2014?

933. The Jack Collins Medal is an award in AFL given to a player or players for what particular achievement?

934. Who was the driver who lost second place in the Australian Formula One Grand Prix in 2014 after he was disqualified?

935. Which Super Rugby team is based in Christchurch
New Zealand?

936. Who was the golfer who won the 2014 LPGA Tours Founders
Cup in Phoenix Arizona in March 2014?

937. Which horse won the 2013 Cox Plate?

938. Which air force has an aerobatic team known as
"The Thunderbirds"?

939. Which NFL team won the Super Bowl in 1986, 1990 and
2007?

940. Up to 2015, what was the highest partnership for
the 1st wicket in a Sheffield Shield/Pura Cup match?

941. How many rugby league test matches did Mal Meninga play
for Australia?

942. What is the name of the Group One race held on the first day
of the Melbourne Spring Carnival at Flemington. A race for
three year old fillies over 2,500 metres; a race which was first
run in 1855?

943. Who won the gold medal for the men's singles tennis at the
1996 Atlanta Olympic Games?

944. Who, in 1892, became the first world heavyweight boxing
champion under Queensbury Rules ?

945. Which three VFA clubs were admitted to the VFL in 1925?

946.   Which English Premier League club is based at Goodison
        Park in Liverpool?

947.   What sport was created in Japan in 1882 by Jigoro Kano?

948.   Which of the following is not an event in the men's heptathlon:
        60 metre, long jump, shot put, 800 metres, 1000 metres, high
        jump and pole vault?

949.   Which country won the women's World Cup of lacrosse in
        1986 and 2005?

950.   At which venue did Australia win back the cricket Ashes in the
        2013 series against England?

951.   Who were the winners of the Laureus World Sports award for
        a team in 2014?

952.   Which team won gold for netball at the 2010 Delhi
        Commonwealth Games?

953.   Who was the woman surfer who won the final of the 2014
        Margaret River APS Pro?

954.   What was the name of the boxer who retained his IBF
        middleweight world boxing title against Australian Anthony
        Mundine at the Sydney Entertainment Centre in January 2013?

955.   Who was appointed captain of the All Blacks rugby union
        side in 2006?

956.   What was the name of the horse that won the 2014 Grand
        National at Aintree in England?

957.　Which horse won the 1890 Melbourne Cup?

958.　Who won the 2012 AFL Brownlow Medal?

959.　Which women's intercolonial sporting event took place for the first between New South Wales and Victoria in 1891?

960.　Who were the two batsmen who scored a partnership of 464 not out for New South Wales against Western Australia in a Sheffield Shield/Pura Cup match in 1990?

961.　How many times did rugby league player Clive Churchill captain Australia?

962.　At which venue is the thoroughbred race, the W.S. Cox Plate, run?

963.　Who was the Australian tennis player who won the men's singles final at the French Championships at Roland Garros in 1966?

964.　Who was the boxer known as "The Manassa Mauler"?

965.　Who was the first St Kilda player to win the Brownlow Medal?

966.　What is the name of the oldest professional association football team in London?

967.　Which horse won the 1891 Melbourne Cup?

968.　In which year was the first Sheffield Shield cricket match played?

969.　Who was the South Sydney rugby league player who scored 29 tries in 19 games during the 1954 season.

970. What feat did George Green achieve as a rugby league player in April 1909?

971. Which NFL team is located in Orchard Park, New York?

972. Who won the 2014 U.S. Masters golf tournament?

973. Which sport did Jack Broughton introduce rules to in 1743 to help prevent the death of competitors?

974. What feat, a first in Australia, did the following women achieve in 1914: Miss L. Noble, Miss A. Noble, Miss E. Keiran and Miss B. Patterson?

975. Which two rugby nations contest the Freedom Cup?

976. In 1915 Isabel Letham became Australia's first female participant in which particular sport?

977. Who was the Australian batsman who scored a century in the last session of the day by hitting a six off the last ball of the day off the bowling of England's Bob Willis during a test match at the WACA ground in Perth in 1974?

978. How old was Australian test cricketer Victor Trumper when he died in 1915?

979. Which radio station in 1924, provided the first sports broadcast in Australia?

980. Up to 2015, what was the record for a tenth wicket partnership in Sheffield Shield/Pura Cup cricket?

981. Wally Lewis captained the Kangaroos on how many occasions?

982. Which horse won the Group One Winterbottom Stakes at Ascot in Perth in 2008?

983. Who was the first tennis player, man or woman , to win all four Grand Slam tournaments in the one year?

984. Who held the world heavyweight boxing title from July 1919 until September 1926?

985. Which AFL club has the motto: *Victoria Amat Curam* (victory demands dedication)?

986. The supporters of which Premier League club in England have been associated with disasters at Heysel Stadium in 1985 and at Hillsborough in 1989?

987. How old was Don Bradman when he scored his first century in cricket?

988. Who was considered by Forbes to be the world's top earning athlete of 2002?

989. Which VFL team received the premiership in 1924 despite losing the final? The VFL had reverted to an unpopular round robin final system at the time.

990. Who was Mark Webber's Red Bull Formula One driving partner for the 2013 season?

991. Which A-League club is affiliated with the Fort Lauderdale Strikers in the U.S.?

992. How many times did West Australian cricketer Terry

Alderman fail to score while playing Sheffield Shield/Pura Cup matches with Western Australia?

993. At which Olympic Games did Taekwondo become a full medal sport?

994. Who were the two Australian women who won gold medals at the 1952 Helsinki Olympic Games?

995. Who was the golfer who took out the first official professional golf championship of Australia when held at the Australia Golf Club in Sydney in 1925?

996. The race horse Hardrada won which Western Australian Group One race in 2002 and 2003?

997. Who won the 2013 Tour de France cycle race?

998. Who was the well known Australian basketball player and coach who played in the Australian football demonstration game during the 1956 Melbourne Olympic Games?

999. What was the nickname of former AFL/VFL footballer Bernie Quinlan ?

1000. Up to 2015, who had played the most Sheffield Shield/Pura Cup cricket matches as a captain?

1001. How many rugby league tours for Australia (Kangaroos) did player Mal Meninga make during his career?

1002   What was the former name of the Crown Oaks horse race
        which is run at Flemington in Melbourne?

1003.   Who was the player who won all four men's tennis Grand Slam
        tournaments in 1962 and again in 1969?

1004.   What do the initials "TKO" mean in the sport of boxing?

1005.   Who was the first coach of the AFL side, the West Coast
        Eagles?

1006.   Which English Premier League club was once known as
        St Mark's and later as Ardwick Association Football Club?

1007.   Who captained-coached VFL/AFL club Geelong to their first
        premiership in 1925?

1008.   Who won the men's 2014 Bell's Beach Surfing Pro?

1009.   Which horse won the 2013 Victoria Derby?

1010.   Who was the winner of the 2014 Formula One Canadian
        Grand Prix?

1011.   Which team defeated Spain 5-1, (World Cup holders), during
        their opening 2014 World Cup game?

1012.   Which NFL team won the Super Bowl in 1972?

1013.   A statue outside the Melbourne Cricket Ground depicting a
        game of football being played by two boys and being

umpired by Tom Wills, is a match between which two schools?

1014.   What feat did Wallabies player Michael Hooper achieve when he replaced Stephen Moore as captain in 2014?

1015.   In which year did the South African rugby team, the Springboks, make their World Cup debut?

1016.   Who, in 1880, designed the first Australian rules football ?

1017.   Which team won the 2012 Western Australian Football League premiership?

1018.   Who captained the Socceroos at the 2014 World Cup?

1019.   Which AFL team used Arden Street Oval as a venue between 1925 and 1985?

1020.   Up until 2015, who had scored the most 100s for New South Wales in Sheffield Shield/Pura Cup matches?

1021.   How many points did rugby league player Michael Cronin score in 22 tests for Australia?

1022.   What weight was carried by the thoroughbred Bernborough when it won the Doomben Cup in 1946?

1023.   Who was the tennis player who won the Wimbledon and U.S. men's singles titles in 2004, 2005, 2006, 2007 and 2008?

1024.   Who was world heavyweight boxing champion from 1937 until 1949?

1025. What position did the Adelaide Crows finish in their first two seasons (1991 and 1992) in the AFL?

1026. Which English Premier League club is based at Old Trafford?

1027. Who won the 2014 women's singles final at the U.S. tennis Open?

1028. Name the jockey that rode the winner of 2014 Caulfield Cup?

1029. How many games did AFL club St Kilda win in succession in 2009?

1030. What motor sport event did Australian Jack Miller win in October 2014?

1031. Who won the men's marathon during the 2012 London Olympic Games?

1032 Which South Australian National Football League club did Brownlow medallist John Platten play with?

1033. What do we call a cricket delivery which, when pitched, spins away from the right handed batsman and is mainly bowled out the back of the hand using the wrist?

1034. In which year was the first "World Series" of American baseball played?

1035. Who was the South African player who scored a drop goal in extra time to enable the Springboks to win the 1995 rugby union World Cup final against New Zealand?

1036. Which horse won the 2014 W.S. Cox Plate ?

1037. What is the series called in baseball when the champions of the American League play the champions of the National League?

1038. Who was the North Melbourne (AFL) player who scored 671 goals for the club between 1989 and 2001?

1039. What was the Australian sporting event won by Ivo Whitton in 1912, 1913, 1926, 1929 and 1931?

1040. How many 100s did Don Bradman score for New South Wales?

1041. How many tries did rugby league player Ken Irvine score in 31 test matches for Australia?

1042. Which horse won the 1946 L.K.S. MacKinnon Stakes after Bernborough was forced out of the race with an injury?

1043. Who was the Australian men's singles tennis player who won the 1933 Australian, French and Wimbledon titles?

1044. Who held the world welterweight boxing title from 1946 to 1951?

1045. Who was the first coach of the AFL's Adelaide Crows?

1046. Which two association football clubs in England play the Tyne-Wear Derby?

1047. In cricket, what is a "brace"?

1048. What part of Australia does tennis player Nick Kyrgios originate from?

1049. Which VFL/AFL team used Brunswick Street Oval as a home venue between 1897 and 1966?

1050. The Trent Bridge ground is the home of which English county cricket club?

1051. Who was the Canterbury Bulldogs player who made 317 appearances for the club between 1996 and 2009?

1052. Who was the player who scored 229 for the Tasmanian Tigers against the Queensland Bulls in a Matador Cup one day match on October 18th 2014?

1053. Who won the AFL's Brownlow Medal in 1993?

1054. What was the name of the Australian Rugby League side formed in 1992 based in Perth?

1055. Who was the captain of the victorious South African rugby union team that won the 1995 World Cup?

1056. How many tries did West Tigers player Taniela Tuiaki score for the club in the 2009 season?

1057. What nationality is golfer, and winner of the 2008 Australian Open, Tim Clark?

1058. Who won the women's singles title at the 2014 French Tennis Open?

1059. Which horse won the 2013 Melbourne Cup?

1060. Who was the New South Wales spin bowler who delivered 26,764 balls in Sheffield Shield/Pura Cup cricket between 1982 and 1997 averaging 28.97?

1061. How many tries were scored by Cecil Blinkhorn on the 1922-23 rugby league "Kangaroos"tour of Great Britain?

1062. In which Queensland town was the racehorse, Bernborough born in 1939?

1063. Who was the first woman to win more than ten Grand Slam tennis titles?

1064. Who was declared World Boxing Council heavyweight champion in 1993?

1065. Who was the first coach of the Brisbane Bears (AFL)?

1066. Which English Premier League team has as its theme song "On the Ball City"?

1067. Which golf tournament did Australian Adam Scott win on August 25th 2013?

1068. What was the original name of the NBLs Adelaide 36s, which were founded in 1982?

1069. Who was the captain of England's women's T20 cricket team that played and lost the final against Australia in the world championship in April 2014?

1070. Who was the coach of the English national rugby union side from 1st July 2008 until November 16th 2011?

1071. Against which team did the West Coast Eagles score a record total of 192 points in 1988?

1072. Who was the British runner who won both the 5,000 and 10,000 metres gold medals at the 2012 London Olympic Games?

1073. Who did Lleyton Hewitt defeat to win the men's singles title at the Brisbane Tennis International in January 2013?

1074. Which NBL team plays their home games at the "Brett Maher Court"?

1075. What is name of the South African premier domestic rugby union competition ?

1076. Which football competition had the following clubs as inaugural members: Albert Park, East Melbourne and Hotham?

1077. Who was the former Australian test cricketer who coached WAFL club Subiaco in 1964, 1965 and 1966?

1078. Which NFL team are known as the "Pats"

1079. Who was the former Richmond (AFL) and South Fremantle player who coached West Perth (WAFL) in 1987 and 1988?

1080. What was cricketer Don Bradman's batting average for South Australia in Sheffield Shield matches?

1081. How many rugby league test caps were earned by Garry Jack of Balmain?

1082. In which year was the first official horse race meeting held in Australia?

1083. Who was the first woman to win all four Grand Slam tennis singles titles in the one year?

1084. Who did Muhammad Ali fight in the "Rumble in the Jungle" match in Zaire (Republic of the Congo) in 1974?

1085. Who was the inaugural coach of the AFL's Brisbane Lions?

1086. Which English Premier League club is based at Loftus Road?

1087. In which year was the first Australian golf Open held?

1088. Who was the athlete who won a silver medal for the men's aerials at the 2014 Sochi Winter Olympic Games?

1089. What feat did sportswoman Jane Tate achieve in 1946?

1090. In which state of Australia would you find the Aussie rules football club known as the Two Wells Roosters?

1091. Who was the Australian batsman who scored 108 against India batting as a night watchman during a match at the WACA ground in Perth during the 1977/78 season?

1092. In which year was the first horse race meeting held in Melbourne?

1093. Which horse won the 1924 Melbourne Cup?

1094. Who was the AFL player who kicked 111 goals for his club in the 1991 AFL season?

1095. What major contribution did William Percy Carpmael make to rugby union?

1096. Who won the Perth International Golf Tournament which was held in October 2014?

1097. Who were the equal winners of the 2013/2014 "Golden Boot" award for the best scorer in European association football?

1098. What is the name of the race day held at Flemington, two days after Melbourne Cup day?

1099. Who was, according to Forbes, the world's richest paid sportsman for 2014?

1100. How many centuries did cricketer Ian Chappell score for South Australia in Sheffield Shield matches?

1101. How many rugby league test caps were earned by Cronulla's Andrew Ettingshausen?

1102. Where did the Australian Jockey Club move its headquarters to after leaving Homebush (1842-1859) in 1860?

1103. Who was the woman who won all four tennis Grand Slams in 1970?

1104. Who was the boxer who knocked out Floyd Patterson to become world heavyweight champion in 1962?

1105. Up to 2015, how many South Australian National Football League premierships had Port Adelaide won?

1106. Which English Premier League club is known as "The Potters"?

1107. Where was the last Formula One motor race held for the 2014 season?

1108. Who was the Canterbury Bulldogs player who scored 159 tries for the club?

1109. Who was the rugby union player who earned 141 international caps; 133 for Ireland and 8 for British and Irish Lions between 1999 and 2014?

1110. Which international club did A-league club Sydney FC play on November 27th 2007 in front of a record crowd of 80,295?

1111. In cricketing terms, what is a "chinaman"?

1112. Which two AFL clubs did Brownlow medallist Shane Woewodin play with?

1113. In which year did Australia play its first Twenty20 international cricket match ?

1114. Who won the men's singles final at the 2014 French Tennis Open?

1115. Who do the Australian, New Zealand and South African touring rugby union teams traditionally play in their last match of their tour of the "Home Nations"?

1116. Who was the West Coast Eagles player who kicked two goals from his first two kicks in the AFL playing in a match against St Kilda in 1992?

1117. What is the name of the event in the Winter Olympic Games where a competitor faces down on a sled and travels down an iced track at speeds of up to 130 kmph?

1118. During an Ashes test in December 1979 Australian fast bowler Denis Lillee, while batting, used an aluminium bat known as a ComBat. The English captain complained to the umpire that the bat was damaging the ball and therefore asked to exchange it for a conventional wooden bat. Who was the English captain who made the complaint?

1119. At which venue did Peter Senior win the 2012 Australian Open golf tournament?

1120. Up to 2015, who had scored the most 100s for Tasmania in Sheffield Shield/Pura Cup matches?

1121. How many Australian rugby league test caps were earned by Wally Lewis?

1122. In which year was the Sydney Turf Club formed?

1123. In which year did tennis player, Margaret Court, win her first Australian Open singles (Australian Championship) title?

1124. Who was heavyweight boxing champion of the world from September 1952 until April 1956?

1125. Who was appointed the inaugural coach of the AFL's Gold Coast Suns?

1126. Which English Premier League club moved from Roker Park to the Stadium of Light in 1997, a place where they now play their home games?

1127. With which sport do we associate the term "the black dot"?

1128. Who was considered by Forbes to be the world's top earning athlete of 1994?

1129.　How many points are scored for a drop goal in rugby union?

1130.　Who was the Australian sports coach who once said "Injuries above the neck don't count"?

1131.　Who did Novak Djokovic defeat to win his first Grand Slam singles title in 2008?

1132.　Who was the Adelaide 36s first coach when they entered the NBL competition in 1982?

1133.　Which AFL/VFL team used Coburg City Oval as a venue in 1965?

1134.　How many goals did Melbourne player Fred Fanning kick in a match against St Kilda in round 19 in 1947?

1135.　In which year did the rugby union team, the Barbarians, play their first match?

1136.　Over what distance is the Bendigo Cup run?

1137.　Who was the Canterbury Bulldogs player who scored 892 goals for the club during his career?

1138.　Which NFL team was founded under the name of the New York Titans?

1139.　Who coached AFL club St Kilda for 332 games?

1140.　How many 100s did Dean Jones score for Victoria in Sheffield Shield/Pura Cup matches?

1141. In which year between 1998 and 2011 did the Brisbane Broncos not appear in the finals?

1142. In which year did the Victorian Jockey Club and the Victoria Turf Club combine to form the Victorian Racing Club?

1143. How many tennis Grand Slam tournaments did American Billy Jean King win in 1972?

1144. What was boxer Muhammad Ali's original name?

1145. Against which two clubs did Essendon win successive VFL/AFL premierships in 1911 and 1912?

1146. Which Welsh club entered the English Premier League (association football) competition in 2011-2012?

1147. Who was the Richmond AFL player who was aged 36 years and 215 days when he played in round 24 for the club 1991?

1148. Who was the Australian athlete who won a bronze medal for the women's freestyle aerial event at the 2014 Sochi Winter Olympic Games?

1149. What is the "Coupe Des Mousquetaires"?

1150. Who was the player won the Wally Lewis Medal for the 2005 State of Origin rugby league series?

1151. Who was runner up to the 2014 AFL Brownlow Medal ?

1152. In which year did Australian motor cycle rider Casey Stoner first win the world MotoGP championship?

1153. How many seasons did Collingwood's Dick Lee top the competitions goal kicking?

1154. Who was the AFL "great" who once said this about Essendon player James Hird." He's a guy that gets up at 6 o'clock in the morning regardless of what time it is"?

1155. Which two rugby union nations compete for the Mandela Challenge Plate?

1156. What is the colour and design of the rugby union team known as the Barbarians?

1157. With which sport is Natalie Medhurst associated?

1158. Who was appointed as Australia's first full time national netball coach in 1990?

1159. How old was Melbourne player Brian Wilson when he won the 1982 VFL/AFL Brownlow Medal?

1160. Up to 2015, who had scored the most 100s for Western Australia in Sheffield Shield/Pura Cup matches?

1161. In which year did the first official match of the World Club Challenge in rugby league take place?

1162. In which year was the South Australian Jockey Club founded?

1163. Who was the woman who won three out of four tennis Grand Slam tournaments in the one year in 1962, 1965, 1969 and 1973?

1164. Who was world heavyweight boxing champion from

September 1926 until July 1928?

1165. In which year was the first Brownlow Medal for the best and fairest player in the AFL/VFL, awarded?

1166. Which two English Premier League teams contest the North London Derby?

1167. Which horse won the 1921 Melbourne Cup?

1168. Who was the former AFL player known as"The Rat"?

1169. Who was the AFL player who was involved in an on field incident which resulted in Hawthorn player Leigh Matthews being charge with assault?

1170. Which English association football club playing in the Championship League is known as the "Tykes"?

1171. Who was the golfer who won the 2014 British Open?

1172. Which former West Coast Eagles player won the Simpson Medal in the 1986 WAFL grand final?

1173. How did Fred Lorz cheat during the 1904 St Louis Olympic Games?

1174. In which year was the Surf Life Saving Association of Australia formed?

1175. In which year did the Australian rugby union team, the Wallabies, become the first team to complete the Grand Slam by defeating England, Wales, Scotland, Ireland and the Barbarians during a tour of the "Home Nations"?

1176. Who was the winner of the Western Australian Football League's Sandover Medal in 2012?

1177. How many goals did John Coleman kick on debut for Essendon against Hawthorn in 1949?

1178. In which year was the inaugural Australian diving championships for men held?

1179. Where, in 1930, did Australia and the West Indies play their first ever cricket test match against each other ?

1180. How many 100s did Tim Zoehrer score for Western Australia in Sheffield Shield/Pura Cup matches?

1181. In which years did the Brisbane Broncos win the World Club Challenge, first against Wigan, and later against the Hunter Mariners?

1182. In which year was the Western Australian Turf Club established?

1183. Who was the woman tennis player who won all four Grand Slam tournaments in 1988?

1184. Who was the World Boxing Council's heavyweight champion from 1978 to 1983?

1185. In which year was the Magarey Medal, the trophy for the fairest and best player in the South Australian National Football League, first awarded?

1186. Which English Premier League team are known as "The Baggies"?

1187. Which horse was "Australian Champion Racehorse of the Year" for three years in a row from 1999-2000 until 2001-2002?

1188. Which team did the Sydney Sixers' defeat to win cricket's Twenty20 Champions League final in 2012?

1189. In which event did Helen Grover and Heather Stanning win Great Britain's first gold medal at the 2012 London Olympics Games?

1190. Which team won the World Netball Championships in 2003?

1191. What is the name of the NFL team located in Baltimore, Maryland USA?

1192. In which year was rugby union's "John Eales Medal" first awarded?

1193. Which horse won the 1925 Melbourne Cup?

1194. Who was the Parramatta Eels player who made 330 appearances for the club between 1998 and 2012?

1195. Who replaced Alan Jones as coach of the Wallabies after the 1987 World Cup?

1196. Who was the Essendon player who made his VFL/AFL debut in 1977 at the age of 15 years and 305 days?

1197. Who was the former Footscray player who was appointed captain coach of West Perth in the WANFL in 1965, winning the Simpson Medal for W.A. against Victoria in the same year?

1198. Which horse won the 2013 Railway Stakes at Ascot racecourse in Perth?

1199. Who was the Melbourne player who won the Coleman Medal in 2002?

1200. Up to 2015, who were the two players who held the record for the 6th wicket partnership in Sheffield Shield/Pura Cup matches?

1201. Who defeated the Brisbane Broncos in a World Club Challenge match in Brisbane in 1994 before a crowd of 54,220?

1202. In which year was the Queensland Turf Club founded?

1203. Who was the woman tennis player who denied Steffi Graf the opportunity of winning all four Grand Slam tournaments in successive years by winning the French Open in 1989?

1204. Who was the American boxer who was the first to win prize money of over $100 million and was also the winner of world titles in five weight divisions?

1205. In which year was the Sandover Medal, a trophy for the fairest and best in the Western Australian Football League, first awarded?

1206. Which English Premier League club, formed in 1932, was admitted to the Premier League in 2011-12?

1207. Who was the Coleman medallist who played for Claremont in their 1964 WANFL premiership team?

1208. Who was the jockey who was disqualified for life (later changed to 5 years) for grabbing the leg of another jockey (Tommy Hill) during the running of the 1961 AJC Derby at Randwick?

1209. Who was the English association footballer who was red carded during a World Cup match against Argentina in 1998?

1210. What is the name of the NFL team located in the city of Cincinnati?

1211. Who was the Argentinian player banned by FIFA for testing positive for the drug ephedrine during the 1994 association football World Cup?

1212. In which year was the inaugural Espirito Santo Trophy awarded; an award presented in a team competition for amateur women golfers?

1213. Where were the Winter Olympic Games held in 1956?

1214. Who is the Western Australian professional golfer nicknamed Rummy?

1215. How many caps did John Eales gain while captain of the Wallabies?

1216. How many times did Trevor Hendy win the Australian "Iron Man" title?

1217. Who coached the Adelaide 36s in the NBL between 2010 and 2013?

1218. Who was the Australian bowler who injured his shoulder while tackling a pitch invader at the WACA ground in Perth during a cricket test match in 1982/83?

1219. Who became Wallabies captain in 1947 at the age of 21 years and 57 days?

1220. What feat did Adam Voges achieve for Western Australia in a Sheffield Shield/Pura Cup match against Queensland in January 2009?

1221. Who were the two veteran players who retired from rugby league after their team, the Brisbane Broncs, won their 5th premiership in 2000?

1222. In which year was the Tasmanian Racing Club established?

1223. Who was the woman tennis player who helped deny Monica Seles the opportunity of winning four Grand Slam tournaments in 1991 and again in 1992, by winning Wimbledon in both those years?

1224. Who were the two boxers who fought "The Thrilla in Manila" in 1975 ?

1225. Up to and including 2015, who are the four players who have won the Brownlow Medal, a trophy for the fairest and best in the AFL, three times?

1226. Which English Premier League team plays at Molineux Stadium?

1227. Who was the North Melbourne player who kicked 14 goals in a match against Melbourne in round 14 of 1990?

1228. West Coast Eagle Scott Cummings kicked a record tally of goals against Adelaide in a match in 2000. How many goals did he kick on that day?

1229. Against which team did Wallaby Matt Hodgson make his test debut?

1230. Who was the motor cycle rider who won five MotoGP championships between 2001 and 2005?

1231. How many goals did St Kilda's Tony Locket kick in a game against Sydney in round 13 in 1992?

1232. Who was the Victorian who led the goal kicking in the WANFL in 1963 while playing for West Perth?

1233. Who was the winner of Australian netball's 2014 Liz Ellis Diamond?

1234. Who was the winner of the 2014 Australian PGA golf tournament?

1235. What do the following rugby union players have in common: Australians John Eales, Tim Horan, Dan Crowley, Jason Little, Phil Kearns and South African Os du Randt?

1236. Who was the surfer who won the 2014 Pipeline Masters?

1237. What does the term "Mankaded" refer to in cricket?

1238. Who was voted FIFA "World Player of the Year" in January 2014?

1239. Who once said, " Baseball has the great advantage over cricket of being sooner ended"?

1240. Who are the two players who have each captained Western

Australia in Sheffield Shield/Pura Cup matches 47 times?

1241. Who won rugby league's Clive Churchill Medal in 1990?

1242. Who was the Australian jockey who rode Ballymoss to victory in the French race, the Prix de l'Arc de Triomphe in 1958?

1243. Who was the tennis player who helped deny Steffi Graf the opportunity of winning all four Grand Slams in 1993 by winning the Australian Open in that same year?

1244. As of 2016, who holds the record as the youngest boxer to hold the WBC, WBA, and the IBF world heavyweight titles?

1245. Up to and including 2015, how many players, excluding those who have won three times, have won the AFL's Brownlow Medal twice?

1246. When was the English Football Association Challenge Cup (FA Cup) first played?

1247. Which horse won the 2013 Caulfield Cup?

1248. Which team won the 2014 FA Cup?

1249. Which AFL club has adopted the term "Shinboner Spirit"?

1250. Who was the snooker player who became the sport's first millionaire, and during the 80's won 6 world championships?

1251. Who was the Parramatta Eels player who scored 2001 points for the club between 1977 and 1986?

1252. In which year did the thoroughbred horse race, the Railway Stakes, change from 1,500 metres to 1,600 metres ?

1253. Who was the player who won the Wally Lewis Medal in the 2007 State of Origin rugby league series?

1254. How many runs did Australian test player Shaun Marsh score on test debut in a match against Sri Lanka in 2011?

1255. John Eales played with which "Super Rugby" club?

1256. Who captained the Melbourne Stars in the Big Bash League during the 2014-15 season?

1257. Who was the British Prime Minister who also played first class cricket?

1258. Which team won the 2013 Ryobi Australian one day cricket cup?

1259. Who was the first Australian rules footballer to receive a Queen's honour?

1260. Up to 2015, who had played the most Sheffield Shield/Pura Cup matches for Western Australia?

1261. Who won rugby league's Clive Churchill Medal in 2009?

1262. Who was the Australian jockey who rode the winner of the Irish Derby in 1947?

1263. In 2002 Jennifer Capriati won the Australian Open singles title. Who was the other player that won the French , U.S. and Wimbledon titles that year?

1264. Who was heavyweight boxing champion of the world from June 1930 until June 1932?

1265. Up to and including 2015, how many AFL Brownlow Medals had been won by Collingwood players?

1266. Which team won the 2011 FA Cup final?

1267. Which horse won the 2012 Geelong Cup?

1268. The winner of which event wins the Vince Lombardi Trophy?

1269. Which team won the 2014 women's Champion's Trophy in hockey, winning the final in a goal shoot out 1-3?

1270. Who was the player who was taken by the Carlton Football Club as number one draft choice in the AFL in 2005?

1271. What is the nickname of the Australian Hockey League's men's team from Queensland?

1272. What feat did cricketer Sam Morris achieve when he took part in the second test of the 1884-85 Ashes series?

1273. Up to and including 2015, how many times had the NFL team, the Cleveland Browns reached the Super Bowl?

1274. Who was the North Melbourne player who won the Tassie Medal in 1958?

1275. Who was the first aboriginal to represent Australia in rugby union?

1276. Who won the Stawell Easter Gift in both 1970 and 1972?

1277. Who was runner up to Novak Djokovic in the men's singles final of the 2013 Australian Tennis Open?

1278. Who was the Raider's back rower who, in 1994, scored the quickest try in a rugby league grand final?

1279. Who is the only player to have played in both a FIFA World Cup tournament and a ICC (cricket) World Cup tournament?

1280. In which year was the Sheffield Shield competition first contested?

1281. Who won rugby league's Clive Churchill Medal in 2011?

1282. Who was the Australian jockey known as "The Enforcer"?

1283. In 2004 Anastasia Myskina (French Open), Maria Sharapova (Wimbledon), and Sventlana Kuznetsova (U.S. Open), were Russians who won three of the Grand Slams that year. Who was the non Russian player who won the fourth Grand Slam, the Australian Open, in 2004?

1284. In which country was world heavyweight boxing champion Tommy Burns born?

1285. Up to and including 2015, how many AFL Brownlow Medals have been won by Carlton players?

1286. Up to and including 2015, which English association football side had won the FA Cup 11 times?

1287. Which cricket team won the 2014 women's World T20 cricket final?

1288. What sporting title was won by Australian Joel Parkinson in December 2012?

1289. Who captained the French side against the Wallabies in the 2014 series in Australia?

1290. Who was the player who put Sydney into the 1996 AFL grand final for the first time in 51 years when he kicked a point from 50 metres out after the siren?

1291. Who coached the Parramatta Eels in 2013?

1292. Who was the South Sydney rugby league player who switched to rugby union by signing with English club Bath in February 2014?

1293. Who was the winner of cricket's Alan Border Medal, announced in January 2014 ?

1294. Who were the two brothers who captained Collingwood in the AFL, the first in 1971 and 1975 and the other brother in 1977?

1295. Who was the rugby union player who represented Australia between 1984 and 1993, was capped 63 times, made captain at the age of 25 and remained as captain for 36 matches? During this time he scored 9 tries.

1296. The Edmonton Oilers are within which division of the Western Conference of the North American National Hockey League?

1297. Who were the two North Melbourne players who won the Norm Smith Medal in 1996 and 1999 respectively?

1298. Who was the Australian paralympian who was ruled out of the 2014 Sochi Winter Olympic Games because of an injury suffered in training just days before competition began ?

1299. Who was the famous golfer who once said, "The more I practice the luckier I get"?

1300. In which year was Queensland admitted to the Sheffield Shield cricket competition?

1301. Which club was rugby league player Allan Langer playing for when he was selected for the 1987 Queensland State of Origin side?

1302. Who was the Australian jockey that rode Light Fingers (1965) and Red Handed (1967) to Melbourne Cup victories?

1303. In 1995 and 1996 Steffi Graf won the U.S. and the Wimbledon women's singles titles. Who were the two players that won the women's Australian Open singles title in each of those years?

1304. Who was the first African-American world heavyweight boxing champion?

1305. Up to 2015, how many AFL Brownlow Medals had been won by Geelong players ?

1306. Up to and including 2015, how many times has Leicester City been runners-up in the FA Cup?

1307. The Rodriguez Shield is an award in which football league. It has been awarded every year since 1957 to the club which has the best seasonal record over three grades.

1308. Who was the player who kicked 90 goals for St Kilda (AFL) during the 2004 season?

1309. How many players scored centuries in the first cricket test, India v Australia in Adelaide in December 2014?

1310. Who won the Australian golf Open in 1951, 1967 and 1972?

1311. Murray the Magpie is the mascot of which NBL team?

1312. How many times did Australian Eddie Charlton win the snooker world championship?

1313. Who was the test cricketer who scored his maiden test century of 365 not out against Pakistan in 1958?

1314. Who was the North Melbourne player who had played a total of 409 games by the end of the 2015 AFL season?

1315. Who was the Wallaby (Australian rugby union) player who scored at total of 911 points between 1984 and 1995?

1316. Who was the West Coast Eagles player who was aged 16 years and 268 days when he first played an AFL game for the club in 1996?

1317. Who captained the Australian Wallabies on 59 occasions between 2001 and 2007?

1318. Who won the women's singles title at the 2016 Australian tennis Open?

1319. In which year did North Melbourne player Noel Teasdale win the Brownlow Medal?

1320. In which year was Western Australia admitted to the Sheffield Shield cricket competition?

1321. Which three clubs did rugby league coach Wayne Bennett play for in the Brisbane rugby league competition?

1322. Who was the Australian jockey who rode Saint Crespin to victory in the 1959 Prix de l'Arc de Triomphe?

1323. In 1997 Martina Hingus won the Australian, U.S. and Wimbledon women's singles tennis titles. Who was the player who won the fourth Grand Slam, the French singles title, that year?

1324. Who was world bantamweight boxing champion from November 1952 until he retired in May 1954?

1325. Up to and including 2015, how many AFL Brownlow Medals had been won by Footscray/Western Bulldog players?

1326. Which Scottish team made the FA Cup final in 1883-84 and again in 1884-5?

1327. Who was runner up to Adam Scott in the 2013 Australian Masters golf tournament?

1328. What is the name of the medal awarded to the best player afield in a South Australian National Football League grand final?

1329. Which team won tennis' 2016 Hopman Cup?

1330. Who was the Australian swimmer who won the gold medal for the men's 200m freestyle at the 1988 Seoul Olympics?

1331. Against which country did Australian cricketer Mitchell Marsh play his first ever test for Australia?

1332. What is the name given to the fourteenth hole at the Augusta National Golf Club course, home of the U.S. Masters?

1333. Who were the two brothers who captained Collingwood; the first between 1979-80 and the second from 1987-93?

1334. Who captained the Sydney Sixers in the Big Bash League during the 2014-15 season?

1335. Which nation won the gold medal for rugby union at the 1920 Olympics in Antwerp and at the 1924 Olympics in Paris?

1336. Which two teams played before a record rugby league crowd of 107,999 at Sydney Olympic Stadium in 1999?

1337. Bernie Ecclestone is the CEO and president of an organisation governing which sport?

1338. Against which club did Wallaby Rodney Blake make his Super Rugby debut ?

1339. In which year was the first VFL/ AFL draft pick?

1340. In which year was Tasmania admitted to the Sheffield Shield cricket competition?

1341. Against which side did rugby league player Allan Langer make his test debut for Australia?

1342. Who was the jockey who rode Elvstroem to victory in the 2004 Caulfield Cup?

1343. Who did tennis player Margaret Court play in the women's singles final at the 1973 Australian Open?

1344. Who was the boxer who defeated Japan's "Fighting Harada" in February 1968 to take the WBC world bantamweight title?

1345 Up to and including 2015, how many AFL Brownlow Medals had been won by St Kilda players?

1346. What nationality were the managers of the 2010 and 2011 FA Cup winning sides, Chelsea and Manchester City?

1347. Who won the 2012 Australian PGA championship?

1348. In which event did Australian Peter Antonie win a gold medal at the 1992 Barcelona Olympic Games?

1349. Who was considered by Forbes to be the world's top earning athlete of 2011?

1350. The 1934 British Empire Games were moved from which city to London because of political reasons?

1351. Who was considered by Forbes to be the world's top earning athlete of 2000?

1352. Who did Victoria Azarenka defeat to win the 2013 Australian Open tennis women's singles final?

1353. What was the nickname given to the 1983 Magarey Medallist, Anthony Antrobus?

1354.   Who was the batsman who scored 28 off one over in the second
        Ashes test in Perth in December 2013?

1355.   What are the positions of the three players who form the front
        line of a rugby union scrum?

1356.   What is the name of the medal awarded to the best and fairest
        player of the rugby league club, South Sydney Rabbitohs?

1357.   Who was the former Collingwood player in the AFL who was
        known as "Pebbles"?

1358.   Which horse won the Newmarket Handicap at Flemington
        in March 2014 ?

1359.   What is the lowest score kicked by St Kilda in an AFL game?

1360.   What connection does Phillip Blashki have with
        Australian cricket?

1361.   Which club did rugby league player Allan Langer captain in
        the English Super League?

1362.   Who was the Australian jockey who was killed in a race fall at
        Maison Lafitte racecourse near Paris on November 7th 1962?

1363.   Who did tennis player Martina Navratilova defeat in the final
        of the following tournaments: Wimbledon 1978, 1979, 1982,
        1984 and 1985?

1364.   Who was the boxer who won the IBF world
        bantamweight title in April 1985, holding it until
        it was vacated in 1987?

1365.   Up to and including 2015, how many AFL Brownlow Medals
        had been won by Sydney Swans/South Melbourne players?

1366.   Which association football team was the first and last to win
        the FA Cup at the Millennium Stadium?

1367.   How many times has a WAFL grand final been held at the
        WACA ground?

1368.   Which team did the Australian women's cricket team defeat to
        win the 2013 women's World Cup?

1369.   In which sporting competition is the Fos Williams Medal
        awarded?

1370.   Australian association footballer Mark Bosnich played with
        which three clubs in England?

1371.   Who captained Western Australia in 10 Sheffield Shield
        matches between 1990 and 1991, and one domestic one day
        match in 1990?

1372.   Who was the runner-up of the 2014 men's Australian Open
        tennis singles final?

1373.   What do we call the cricket delivery which when pitched,
        breaks to the left of a right handed batsman and the spin of
        which is produced mainly using the fingers?

1374.   How many times has former Carlton and Port Adelaide player
        Craig Bradley won the Fos Williams Medal ?

1375.   Which position players are usually the tallest in a rugby union
        team?

1376. Who was the Australian rugby league player known as "The Zip Zip Man"?

1377. Ruckman Len Thompson played with which three AFL sides ?

1378. English test batsman Graham Gooch played with which English county club?

1379. Who was the AFL player who won the "Rising Star" award in 1996?

1380. Up to 2015, how many Sheffield Shield/Pura Cup titles had New South Wales won?

1381. What age was rugby league player Allan Langer when he played his final season in 2002?

1382. Who was the jockey who rode the following horses to Melbourne Cup wins: Think Big (twice), Hyperno, and Arwon?

1383. Who did tennis player Serena Williams defeat to win the following singles finals: 2002 French Open, 2002 Wimbledon, 2002 U.S. Open and 2003 Australian Open?

1384. Who was the light heavyweight boxer who knocked out Jimmy Corbett in 1897 to win the world heavyweight title?

1385. Up to and including 2015, how many AFL Brownlow Medals had been won by Melbourne players?

1386. Up to and including 2015, which is the only non English club to have won the FA Cup?

1387. Over what distance is the Victoria Derby run at Flemington ?

1388. Which major sporting event did Ossie Pickworth win in 1946, 1947, 1948 and 1954?

1389. Who was the Hawthorn player who kicked the winning goal after the siren to put his team into the AFL/VFL Grand Final of 1987?

1390. How many world titles did Australian boxer Danny Green win during his career?

1391. Who won the Laureus World Sports award for men in 2011?

1392. In which year did racehorse Briseis win the Melbourne Cup?

1393. In which sport was Harriet Elphinstone Dick famous in both Australia and England during the later part of the 19th century?

1394. In which sport did Paralympian Troy Andrews compete at the Seoul, Barcelona, Atlanta and Sydney Games?

1395. What position player usually takes the throw in at a line-out during a rugby union match?

1396. What is the Jack Oatey Medal awarded for in Aussie Rules ?

1397. What was the name of the horse which won the 2014 Melbourne Cup?

1398. Which team won the first ever Australian women's cricket championship which was played in 1931?

1399. Which Australian club contested the first FIFA Club World Cup?

1400. Which team won the Sheffield Shield/Pura Cup title in 1995-96?

1401. Who was the rugby league player who played 349 games between 1980 and 1996, scored 164 tries, played for New South Wales in the State of Origin and also represented Australia?

1402. Who was the jockey that rode the 1952 Melbourne Cup winner, Dalray?

1403. In which year did tennis player Roger Federer first win a men's singles French Open title?

1404. Who was the boxer who became heavyweight champion of the world by knocking out world title holder Bob Fitzsimmons in Brooklyn New York in 1899?

1405. Up to and including 2015, how many AFL Brownlow Medals had been won by West Coast Eagles players?

1406. What was the first club to win the FA Cup at the new Wembley Stadium?

1407. Against which team did St Kilda score a club record of 204 points at the MCG in 1978?

1408. Who was the AFL coach who was sacked by his club after they were defeated by Greater Western Sydney in a round in 2012?

1409. Which team won the world amateur golf championship for women in Karuizawa Japan in 2014?

1410. Which club of the English Championship League has supporters known as "Bluenoses"?

1411. In which two consecutive years did Mia Hamm (U.S.A.) win the world's best female association footballer of the year award?

1412. What is the name given to the sixth hole at the Augusta National Golf Club course, home of the U.S Masters?

1413. What first did Ernie Bromley achieve when he first played test cricket for Australia in the fourth test of the 1932-33 Ashes series?

1414. How old was Cameroon's Roger Milla when he became the oldest player to score a goal and play in a World Cup during the tournament in 1994?

1415. Who was the rugby union player who played for the Blues, Hurricanes and Chiefs in the Super League, been capped 63 times for New Zealand between 1994 and 2002 and has scored 15 tries in World Cup matches?

1416. What was the name of the super maxi yacht that won the 2012 Sydney to Hobart in record time?

1417. What was West Indian test cricketer Viv Richards highest score in test cricket?

1418. Who was the tennis player who was runner-up in the U.S. Open men's singles final in September 2012?

1419. How many goals did French striker Just Fontane score in the 1958 World Cup tournament, a feat which earned him the

Golden Boot award for that tournament?

1420. Who were the two players who won the Sheffield Shield/Pura Cup competition "Player of the Year" award in 1975-76?

1421. Who was the rugby league player who played 216 games for the Parramatta Eels, was a member of the inaugural State of Origin team for New South Wales and represented Australia 33 times between 1973 and 1982?

1422. Who trained the following horses: Tulloch, Kingston Town, Gynsynd, Redcraze and Red Anchor?

1423. In which year did Rafael Nadal first win a Wimbledon singles title?

1424. Up to 2015, how many times has Everton been runners-up in the FA Cup?

1425. Up to and including 2015, how many AFL Brownlow Medals have been won by Adelaide players?

1426. Who was the inaugural winner of the Fos Williams Medal?

1427. How many times did Kevin Bartlett win the Richmond (AFL) fairest and best award?

1428. Who was the golfer who won the Australian Women's Open at Royal Canberra in 2013?

1429. Australian test cricketer Geoff Marsh made his test debut in 1985 playing against which team?

1430. With which sport were the Danish world champions Erik Gundersen and Hans Nielsen associated?

1431. Who captained the Melbourne Renegades in the Big Bash League during the 2014-15 season?

1432. At which cricket ground would you find the Pavilion End and the Radcliffe Road End?

1433. Which rac horse won both the Winterbottom Stakes and the Railway Stakes in 2003?

1434. Who was the Russian footballer who scored a record 5 goals for a match in a World Cup tournament playing against Cameroon in 1994?

1435. What rugby union concept was conceived in Melrose, Scotland in 1883?

1436. In which season did West Indian cricketer Viv Richards play for Queensland in the Sheffield Shield competition?

1437. Who won the Laureus World Sports award for men in 2006?

1438. What is the name of the netball side out of Adelaide which plays in the Trans Tasman Netball League?

1439. Which air force has an aerobatic team known as "The Black Cats"?

1440. Which three states did Trevor Chappell play for in the Sheffield Shield/Pura Cup competition?

1441. Which English club did Manly-Warringah's Graham Eadie play with between 1986 and 1989?

1442. Who won the Sydney '"Horse Trainers Premiership" every year between 1953 and 1985?

1443. Who won the Australian, French and Wimbledon men's single title in 1956?

1444. Who did Jack Dempsey defeat in July 1919 to take the world heavyweight boxing title?

1445. Up to and including 2015, how many AFL Brownlow Medals had been won by Essendon players?

1446. Which five association football national sides had Guus Hiddink managed between 1994 and 2011?

1447. What was the name of the New Zealand jockey who was killed in a race fall riding Elleaye in the seventh race at Kurow in North Otago in December 2012?

1448. Which two U.S. Major Baseball teams played a series of historic matches at the Sydney Cricket Ground in March 2014?

1449. Who was the Australian rugby league player who captained Halifax to a Challenge Cup victory in 1986-87?

1450. Which country lifted a 50 year pro sports ban from January 2014?

1451. Which A-league club was coached by Rini Coolen between July 2010 and December 2011?

1452. Who was the first Australian to score a goal in an association football World Cup match?

1453. What is the name of the home ground of the Yorkshire County Cricket Club?

1454. With which sport is Olympian Ramon Andersson associated?

1455. Up to and including 2015, how many times had Fiji won the Hong Kong Sevens rugby union tournament?

1456. Who was the Australian sportsman known as "Dr Teeth"?

1457. Who was the AFL player who won the Coleman Medal and kicked 100 goals in three successive seasons (1993, 1994 and 1995)?

1458. With which sport was Olympic gold medallist John Edward Anderson associated?

1459. Who was the former Essendon and Adelaide AFL player who won the 1986 Magarey Medal?

1460. Who was the cricketer who scored 437 for Victoria against Queensland at the Melbourne Cricket Ground in 1927-28?

1461. Who was the Sydney Rooster's rugby league player who became the competition's leading points scorer in 1998 with 284 points?

1462. Who trained Might and Power to victory in the Melbourne Cup, Caulfield Cup and Cox Plate?

1463. Which country won the Davis Cup tennis tournament each year from 1927 to 1932?

1464. Which English association football club won two FA Cups in succession in 1961 and 1962 and again in 1981 and 1982?

1465. Up to and including 2015, how many AFL Brownlow Medals had been won by Brisbane Bears/Brisbane Lions/Fitzroy players?

1466. Who won the first Stawell Easter Gift in 1878?

1467. Who won the Big Bash League's "Player of the Tournament" award in 2014?

1468. How many individual gold medals has American swimmer Michael Phelps won in Olympic Games competition?

1469. Who was the swimmer who defeated Australian James Magnussen by 1/100 of a second to win gold in the 100 metres freestyle at the 2012 London Olympic Games?

1470. In which country is the association football club known as Galatasaray?

1471. Who was the driver who won the 2014 "Bathurst 1000" motor race?

1472. Which horse won the 1922 Melbourne Cup?

1473. Who was the player who won the Wally Lewis Medal in the 2006 State of Origin rugby league series?

1474. In which country was former Liverpool player Craig Johnston born?

1475. Who captained England's rugby union team between 1988 and 1996?

1476. Who was the AFL St Kilda player who captained the side on 177 occasions'?

1477. Over what distance is the Caulfield Guineas run?

1478. In which year did Australia compete in the Davis Cup tennis tournament for the first time as a single nation without New Zealand ?

1479. Which two Tasmanian football clubs did Hawthorn great, Peter Hudson play with?

1480. Up until 2015, who had taken the most wickets in a Sheffield Shield/Pura Cup season?

1481. Who was the indigenous Australian rugby league player who once kicked five field goals in eleven minutes in a game for South Sydney against Penrith in 1969?

1482. Who was the Australian horse trainer who won the King Stand Stakes at England's Royal Ascot with Miss Andretti in 2007?

1483. Who defeated Spain in the 2003 Davis Cup tennis final?

1484. Who was the manager of Arsenal in their 4 FA Cup wins of 1998, 2002, 2003 and 2005?

1485. Up to and including 2015, how many AFL Brownlow Medals have been won by Hawthorn players?

1486. Who captained the Australian Wallabies on 55 occasions between 1996 and 2001?

1487. Who, in 1931, did Australia play in the first cricket test match played at the Gabba ?

1488. Who was the inaugural winner of South Sydney Rabbitoh's George Piggins Medal awarded in 2003?

1489. Which team did cricketer Viv Richards make his test debut against in 1974?

1490. What sporting equipment was invented by Coburn Haskell in 1898?

1491. Who was Stephen Harold Gascoigne?

1492. Which team were minor AFL premiers in 1991?

1493. Which A-league club has a supporter group known as "The Cove"?

1494. How many goals did Hungary score against El Salvador on June 5th 1982 in Elche Spain, recording the biggest score in association football World Cup finals.

1495. Who was the Springbok rugby union player who played a record 102 times for South Africa between 1997 and 2008, scoring a total of 893 points? He was also the leading points scorer in the 2007 World Cup.

1496. DeAndre Daniels, basketball player with the Perth Wild Cats, was recruited from the U.S. signing with the Wild Cats in August 2014. Which team had he been selected for during the 2014 NBA draft in June 2014 ?

1497. Who became Wallabies captain at the age of 23 years and 249 days in 2011?

1498. Who was the coach of the A-League side Adelaide United during the 2014-15 season?

1499 Who was the A-league player who won the "Goalkeeper of the Year" award in 2012-13?

1500. Which state won cricket's Sheffield Shield competition for 9 consecutive years from 1953-4 to 1961-2?

1501. Which Eastern Suburbs rugby league player was known as the "Bradman of the League"?

1502. Who trained the 1980 Melbourne Cup winner Beldale Ball?

1503. In which year did Russia win the Davis Cup (tennis) for the first time?

1504. Who was the manager of Manchester United when they won FA Cup victories in 2004, 1999, 1996, 1994 and 1990?

1505. Up to and including 2015, how many AFL Brownlow Medals have been won by Richmond players?

1506. Who was the Australian basketballer who was traded to the Toronto Raptors in 2010 and later to the New Orleans Hornets in 2010-2011?

1507. Who won the women's singles tennis final at the 2014 Japanese Open?

1508. Name the two competing horses that died after the running of the 2014 Melbourne Cup?

1509. Unley Oval is the home ground of which SANFL team?

1510. Who was the golfer who won the 2014 Australian Open?

1511. In which Australian city was racing car driver Marcos Ambrose born?

1512. Who captained the successful English team on their 1970-71 Ashes cricket tour of Australia?

1513. Who coached St Kilda (AFL) for 121 matches?

1514. Which NBL team did Matt Burston play with during the 2014-15 season?

1515. Up to 2014 Commonwealth Games, how many gold medals had New Zealand won for Rugby Sevens at the Commonwealth Games?

1516. Where was the World Hockey Cup for men held in 2014?

1517. Who was the player who won the AFL's "Rising Star" award for 2012?

1518 What is the weight division in boxing for participants 90.7kg plus?

1519. What is the official nickname of the Australian Under 17 association football team?

1520. In which year did Queensland win cricket's Sheffield Shield for the first time?

1521. How many times did rugby league player Ken Irvine play for Australia?

1522. Who trained the 1991 Australia Cup winner, Better Loosen Up?

1523. Who did Spain defeat to win the 2011 Davis Cup tennis tournament?

1524. Which association football club in England won three FA Cups under manager Bill Nicholson?

1525. Up to and including 2015, how many AFL Brownlow Medals had been won by North Melbourne players ?

1526. Who won the Australian Roxy Pro surf tournament on the Gold Coast in March 2014?

1527. Who succeeded Gold Coast Suns (AFL) coach Guy McKenna in 2014?

1528. Who captained the successful European team which won golf's 2012 Ryder Cup?

1529. In what location in Japan did the martial art of karate first develop?

1530. Who won the MotoGP championship in 1987?

1531. What was the name of the jockey who rode the 2014 Melbourne Cup winner, Protectionist?

1532. What is the name of the medal awarded to the fairest and best player in a Fremantle/West Coast Eagles "Derby" in the AFL?

1533. Where were the Winter Olympic Games held in 1980?

1534. Who was the former St Kilda player who coached WAFL club Subiaco to a premiership in 1973?

1535. Which team defeated South Africa to win the London Rugby Sevens Cup at Twickenham in May 2010?

1536. Who was Australia's first T-20 captain?

1537. Who did Michael Hooper replace as Wallabies captain in 2014?

1538. Who was the first player to get a duck in test cricket?

1539. In which sport did aboriginal Johnny Mullagh excel during the 1870's?

1540. Which state won cricket's Sheffield Shield in the second year of the competition?

1541. Who was the Australian rugby league player who broke his leg against France in 1968, ending his test career?

1542. Who trained the following Golden Slipper winners: Ha Ha(2001), Dance Hero (2004) and Sebring (2008)?

1543. Which country defeated Australia in the Davis Cup tennis final of 1993?

1544. Who was the Arsenal player who made 722 first team appearances for the club between 1975 and 1993?

1545. Up to and including 2015, how many AFL Brownlow Medals have been won by Port Adelaide players?

1546. What sporting event presents the "Joe Kirkwood Cup" to the winner?

1547. What do the following Australian test cricketers have in common: Billy Murdoch (1880), Harry Trott (1896), Monty Noble (1903), Clem Hill (1910), Warwick Armstrong (1920), Lindsay Hassett (1949), Greg Chappell (1975), Graham Yallop (1978) and Steve Smith (2014)?

1548. Who was the player who wore the St Kilda jumper number 35 for 379 games?

1549. What sport was created by Jigoro Kano in 1882?

1550. Which NFL team plays its home games at the Hubert H. Humphrey Metrodome in Minnesota?

1551. What sporting feat was achieved by the following Australian men in 2012: Aron Sherriff, Mark Casey, Brett Wilkie and Wayne Ruediger?

1552. Who once said "Football is all very well a good game for rough girls but not for delicate boys"?

1553. Who rode Gatewood to win the 2012 Geelong Cup?

1554. Why was undefeated world IBF Junior Welterweight champion

Terry March forced to retire in 1987?

1555. Which team won the 2011 USA Sevens Cup rugby union tournament?

1556. Grete Waitz of Norway won a major world sporting event 9 times beginning in 1978 and with her final victory in 1988. What was the event?

1557. In which year was the Port Adelaide Football club founded?

1558. What did the following athletes have in common:
George Parker, Edwin Carr Snr, Bobby Peace, Boy Charlton, Dunc Gray, Les Mckay, Mervyn Wood, Jock Sturrock, Ivan Lund, Bill Roycroft, Dennis Green, Raelene Boyle, Denise Robertson-Boyd, Max Metzker, Wayne Roycroft, Rick Charlesworth, Jenny Donnet, Andrew Hoy, Andrew Gaze, Colin Beashel, James Tomkins and Lauren Jackson?

1559. Who was the South Sydney rugby league player who scored 29 points in a match against Eastern Suburbs in 1952?

1560. In which year was the first Boxing Day cricket test?

1561. In 2004 Manly rugby league player, Steve Menzies broke an eighty year record for the most tries scored by a forward which was previously 146. Whose record did Menzies break?

1562. Who was the trainer of Archer, the horse which won the first two Melbourne Cups, run in 1861 and 1862?

1563. The Davis Cup of tennis was first conceived in 1899 by which university tennis team?

1564. What do the following English national team footballers have in common? David Beckham, Bobby Moore, Bobby Charlton, Peter Shilton and Billy Wright ?

1565. Up to and including 2015, how many AFL Brownlow Medals had been won by Fremantle Dockers players?

1566. Who was named head coach of the Australian netball team in 2011?

1567. Who was considered by Forbes to be the world's top earning athlete of 2007?

1568. What famous Australian racehorse was sired by Bel Esprit in 2006?

1569. Who won the women's singles final of the Brisbane International tennis tournament in 2015?

1570. Who was the former Davis Cup tennis player who won the federal seat of Bennelong at the 2010 federal Australian election?

1571. Which horse won the 2015 "Magic Millions"?

1572. The Bathurst 1000 motor race was first known by what other name?

1573. Which nation won the 2015 Hopman Cup tennis tournament in Perth?

1574. What is the name of the Women's Basketball League team based in Adelaide in 2015?

1575.	Where was the first Australian "Sevens" rugby union tournament held in 2000?

1576.	Which former AFL player and coach once said " Winners are grinners and losers can please themselves"?

1577.	Who did Roger Federer team up with to win a gold medal for the men's doubles at the 2008 Beijing Olympic Games?

1578.	Which Big Bash team did the following overseas players play for during the 2014-15 season: Johan Botha, Kieron Pollard and Ryan Ten Doeschate?

1579.	Which sports league has the following teams as members: Houston Dash, Chicago Red Stars and the Washington Spirit?

1580.	Who won the second Boxing Day cricket test which was played in 1952?

1581.	How many rugby league grand final victories did Norm Provan achieve as coach of St George?

1582.	Which New Zealand bred horse won the Melbourne Cup, Caulfield Cup and Cox Plate in 1954?

1583.	Who won the gold medal for the men's singles tennis at the 1896 Athens Olympic Games?

1584.	Who was the English association footballer who scored 49 goals for England during his career?

1585.	Up to and including 2015, how many AFL Brownlow Medals had been won by Gold Coast Suns players?

1586. Where would you find Australia's National Sports Museum?

1587. How many grand final appearances have both Kevin Walters and Michael Hancock each made for the Brisbane Broncos?

1588. Which horse won the 2012 "Crown Oaks" at Flemington?

1589. Who was the player voted fairest and best for the West Coast Eagles in 2014?

1590. What is the name of the NFL team that is located in Georgia in the U.S.?

1591. What is the nickname of the Australian Hockey League women's team from South Australia?

1592. Who were the five players who each scored a century in the first cricket test of a series between Australia and South Africa in Brisbane in November 2012?

1593. Which NBL team did Lucas Walker play with during the 2014-15 season?

1594 As of 2015, who has been the shortest player to play in the NBA?

1595. Which team won the Dubai Sevens Cup rugby union tournament in 2010?

1596. What sporting event was held on the River Thames in London for the first time in 1829 ?

1597. Which team won rugby union's 2012 Six Nations Championship?

1598. A statue in Fremantle depicting a high mark taken by Western Australian Aussie rules great John Gerovich was modelled on an actual mark taken by Gerovich in 1956. Who was the player who Gerovich marked over?

1599. Who scored 111 for Australia in the third Ashes test at the WACA ground in Perth in December 2013?

1600. Who was the Australian bowler who took 8 for 71 in the Boxing Day cricket test of 1968?

1601. Why did rugby league's St George player Brian Clay miss the 1962 and 1963 grand finals?

1602. How many times did thoroughbred Kingston Town win the W.S.Cox Plate?

1603. Who won the gold medal for women's singles in tennis at the 1900 Paris Olympic Games?

1604. Which VFL(AFL) team failed to win a game in 1964?

1605. Who was the English national goalkeeper who played 23 games for Chesterfield, 293 for Leicester City and 194 for Stoke City?

1606. Who was the Canterbury prop who was charged with biting the ear of Melbourne Storm's Billy Slater in the 2012 rugby league grand final?

1607. In which year was the first English Grand National horse race run?

1608. Which team was runner-up in the 2014 "Big Bash" cricket final?

1609.   In which year was the first Boston marathon run?

1610.   Who was the South Sydney rugby league player who once kicked 112 goals and 19 field goals in a season for the club?

1611.   Who was the batsman who scored 209 in a cricket test match at the Bellerive Oval in Tasmania in January 2010?

1612.   Who captained AFL club St Kilda for 83 games?

1613.   Who was the golfer who won the 2014 women's U.S. Open?

1614.   What name is given to the fifteenth hole at the Augusta National Golf Club course, home of the U.S. Masters?

1615.   Which Asian team competed in the Australian National Basketball League in 2006-2007 and 2007-2008?

1616.   Who once said, " Golf is a good walk spoiled"?

1617.   How many sailors lost their lives in the 1998 Sydney to Hobart yacht race?

1618.   In which NSW town was former North Melbourne (AFL) player Wayne Carey born?

1619.   Where was the world speedway championship venue between the years 1936 and 1960?

1620.   Who were the two Australians who made centuries in the Boxing Day cricket test of 1975?

1621. Who was the St George rugby league player who was the competition's leading try scorer in 1958 and 1962?

1622. What do the following racehorses have in common: Phar lap, Flight, Tobin Bronze, Sunline, Northerly and Fields of Omagh?

1623. Todd Woodbridge and Mark Woodforde won medals for men's doubles tennis at the Atlanta Olympic Games in 1996 and at the Sydney Olympics in 2000. What medals were awarded to them in each of these games?

1624. Which team in the VFL (AFL) were once known as the Gorillas?

1625. Who was the English association footballer who was awarded the "Golden Boot" in the 1986 World Cup?

1626. Who was the Melbourne Tigers basketball player who scored 50 points in a match against the Sydney Kings at the Hisense Arena in March 2014?

1627. Who won the 2013 Stawell Easter Gift?

1628. Which race team did Formula One driver Lewis Hamilton leave in 2012 to join the Mercedes works team in 2013?

1629. Who was the first woman to fly solo around Australia?

1630. Which NBL team did Alex Pledger play with during the 2014-15 season?

1631. Which football team won the 2013 American Super Bowl?

1632. What was or is a "Stade"?

1633. What is the oldest continental association football world championship?

1634. Against which team did cricketer Sachin Tendulkar make his test debut in 1989?

1635. What was the original name of the Australian Basketball League side the Adelaide 36's when they first joined the competition in 1982?

1636. Which horse won the 1931 Melbourne Cup?

1637. Who was the Western Australian golfer who was awarded the silver trophy for the best placed amateur at the U.S. Masters in 2014?

1638. Where is the Victorian Golf Club located, a past venue for the Australian Open tournament?

1639. What is the nickname of the Australian Hockey League women's team from Tasmania?

1640. Who was "Man of the Match" in the 1980 Boxing Day cricket test?

1641. What is the name of the trophy which is competed for between rugby league teams South Sydney and the Sydney Roosters?

1642. What do the following horses have in common: Makybe Diva, Might and Power, Saintly, Nightmarch, Phar Lap and Raising Fast?

1643.	In which year was the "Federation Cup" of tennis launched?

1644.	Who was the heavyweight boxing champion who was known as "The Brown Bomber"?

1645.	Who was the Fitzroy player in the VFL who played a total of 333 VFL games, represented Victoria 24 times, represented Western Australia 6 times and played for East Perth in the Western Australian National Football League, playing 44 games for that club as captain coach?

1646.	Who was the youngest member of England's 1966 association football World Cup winning team?

1647.	What was the nickname of former Penrith Panthers and Auckland Warriors captain Greg Alexander?

1648.	Why was Australian test cricketer Terry Alderman banned from international cricket for three years, disqualifying him from taking part in the 1985 Ashes series against England?

1649.	Who won "Player of the Series" in the Ashes cricket series played in Australia in 2013-14?

1650.	Who won the "Laureus World Sportsman Award" for 2014?

1651.	What is known as the "Devil's Number" in cricket?

1652.	Which South Australian National Football League club was coached by Haydn Bunton Junior from 1975 to 1982?

1653.	With which sport is Australian Dianne Alagich associated?

1654. Who was the player who captained the NBL's Adelaide 36s for 13 seasons between 1997 and 2009?

1655. In which season did the Cairns Taipans first enter the Australian National Basketball League?

1656. Which horse won the 2015 Perth Cup?

1657. Who was the St Kilda AFL player who played 123 consecutive games for the club?

1658. What award was won by West Coast Eagles player Andrew Gaff in 2015?

1659. Who won the women's singles final at the 2013 French tennis Open?

1660. In which year did Australian cricketer Graham Yallop score 268 during a Boxing Day test against Pakistan?

1661. Who was the rugby league player who coached the following teams between 1969 and 1978 : Kurri Kurri, Newtown Jets, Wests (Newcastle), St George, and Cronulla-Sutherland?

1662. In which year was the first W.S. Cox Plate horse race run?

1663. Which country won the Federation Cup of tennis in 2011?

1664. Against which club did Fitzroy play their last AFL game in 1996?

1665. Who was the English association footballer who gained 63 caps for England and played for Scunthorpe United, Liverpool, Hamburger SV, Southampton and Newcastle United? He also spent time as a manager of Newcastle United, Fulham, Manchester City and the England national side.

1666. Who was the first number one draft pick to win the Brownlow Medal in the AFL?

1667. What is the nickname of the Australian Hockey League men's team from South Australia?

1668. Who were the two players who captained the Western Australian State of Origin football side in matches played in 1985?

1669. Which South Australian National Football League club did 1981 Magarey Medallist, Michael Aish play with between 1979 and 1993?

1670. Which two leagues make up American Major League baseball?

1671. What number guernsey was worn by Collingwood player Darren Millane? The guernsey was "retired "after his death in 1991.

1672. Against which team did Wallaby Clyde Rathbone play his first test for Australia?

1673. What is the name of the NFL team that is located in North Carolina in the U.S.?

1674. Who was the cyclist who won the gold medal for Australia in the Madison event at the 2000 Sydney Olympic Games?

1675. In which season did the Australian National Basketball League team, the Gold Coast Blaze, join the competition?

1676. Which club did Japanese player Shinji Ono join in the Australian A-League in 2012?

1677. What nationality is world sprint champion Usain Bolt?

1678. What is the nickname of the Australian Hockey League women 's team from Victoria?

1679. Which horse won the Melbourne Cup in 1932?

1680. Who was the 18 year old Australian bowler took 6 wickets on debut in 1984 against the West Indies?

1681. Who was the rugby league player who played for South Sydney and Manly Warringah, first played for New South Wales in 1967 and had the nickname of "Lurch"?

1682. How many consecutive races did the horse "Ajax" win?

1683. Which country won 7 consecutive tennis Federation Cups between 1976 and 1982?

1684. Who was the VFL/AFL leading goal scorer for five years in succession, between 1949-1953?

1685. Who was the English association footballer who made his debut in 1988, played a total of 559 games playing for Southampton, Blackburn Rovers and Newcastle United, represented England 63 times and scored 30 goals for his country. He captained England in 1996.

1686. Who was the female gymnast who was known as the "Sparrow from Minsk" ?

1687. Who was the English batsman who became the first cricketer to reach 100 tests?

1688. Who was the rider who took first place at the 2012 Portuguese MotoGP ?

1689. Which team won the first Asian Cup of association football, played in 1956?

1690. In which sport would you find an oxer?

1691. Who was the first woman to swim under one minute for the 100 metres freestyle?

1692. Which team in the Women's Basketball League was coached by Kennedy Kereama in 2015?

1693. The 2014 Winter Olympic Games were held in the Russian city of Sochi which is on the shore of which sea?

1694. How many State of Origin matches did John Todd coach Western Australia in between 1983 and 1988?

1695. What is the oldest team in the Australian National Basketball League?

1696. What feat was achieved by Gerd von Dincklage-Schulinburg on January 24th 1956?

1697. In which year was the English Premier League first introduced?

1698.   What is the weight of a shot put in men's open competition?

1699.   Former heavy weight boxing champion Joe Louis attempted a comeback after he vacated the heavyweight title in 1949. Who were two boxers he fought and failed against in an attempt to win back the title?

1700.   Who scored 105 for Australia in the Boxing Day cricket test of 1997?

1701.   Who was the rugby league and rugby union Australian representative known as "Mr Perpetual Motion"?

1702.   Who rode the rac horse Ajax in 37 races, for 30 wins, 5 seconds and 2 thirds?

1703.   Which country was runner-up on 6 consecutive occasions in the Federation Cup of tennis?

1704.   On how many occasions did Gordon Coventry top the goal scoring list for the VFL/AFL?

1705.   Who was the English association footballer who made his debut for Newcastle United in 1985, played for England 57 times and scored 10 goals. In his total of 391 senior appearances he represented Newcastle United, Tottenham Hotspur, Everton and Middlesborough as well as Italian club Lazio, Scottish club Rangers, Burnley, Gansu Tianma in China and Boston United.

1706.   Who was the Australian who scored 156 off 63 balls in a twenty20 international against England in 2013?

1707.   What is the national summer sport of Canada?

1708. With which sport is Australian Heinrich Haussler associated?

1709. Australian Nick A'Hern is associated with which sport?

1710. In which year was the first "City to Surf" held in Perth?

1711. What was the third Formula One Grand Prix of 2013?

1712. Who was the journalist who is credited with labelling the Australian soccer team as "the Socceroos" in 1967?

1713. What do the following test cricketers have in common: Reginald Foster (England), Lawrence Rowe (West Indies), Brendon Kuruppu (Sri Lanka), Matthew Sinclair (NZ) and Jacques Rudolph (South Africa)?

1714. Who was coach of the A-League side Sydney FC during the 2014-15 season?

1715. What is the name of the New Zealand team that competes in the Australian National Basketball League?

1716. Where was former Collingwood full forward Brian Taylor recruited from in 1980?

1717. Who was the West Coast Eagles player who won the Simpson Medal in the 2000 WAFL grand final?

1718. How many games did AFL club St Kilda loose in succession from round one 1897 until round 17 1899?

1719. What feat did Australian cricketer Warren Barnsley achieve in the fifth test at the Oval against England in August 1909?

1720. Who took his 300th test wicket on the final day of the 1988 Boxing Day cricket test?

1721. How many tries did Glenn Lazarus score for New South Wales in rugby league State of Origin matches between 1989 and 1999?

1722. Which horse suffered a broken pelvis during the 1979 Melbourne Cup and had to be put down?

1723. Which two nations fought out the first tennis Federation Cup in 1963?

1724. Who was the Collingwood player in the VFL/AFL who topped the goal kicking list eight times between 1907 and 1919?

1725. Who was the knighted English association footballer who was the first winner of the "European Footballer of the Year" and "Football Writer's Association Footballer of the Year"?

1726. Who was "Australian International Netball Player of the Year" for 2014?

1727. What nationality is pro surfer Adriano De Souza?

1728. Who was the Australian who won four gold and four silver Olympic medals between 1956 and 1964?

1729. How many wickets did Australian Nathan Lyon take in total in the first test against India in Adelaide in December 2014?

1730. Which A-league team awards the "Gary Wilkins Medal"?

1731. Old Trafford cricket ground is the home of which English county cricket club?

1732. Who was the first person to break the one minute barrier for the 100 metres freestyle swim?

1733. Which horse won the 2015 Melbourne Cup?

1734. Who was the first cricketer to score 400 runs in a test innings?

1735. What was the original name of the Australian Basketball League team, the Perth Wildcats?

1736. What feat was achieved by Lesley Cherriman on April 13th 1969?

1737. Which team won the 2012-13 Sheffield Shield cricket competition?

1738. Who was the Kenyan runner who won the gold medal and broke the world record for the 800 metres at the London Olympics in 2012?

1739. Who won the individual title for the World Cup of Golf in 2013?

1740. Who made his test debut for Australia in the Boxing Day test of 1985?

1741. Who coached the South Sydney Rabbitohs from 1962 to 1966?

1742. Who rode Melbourne Cup winners Just a Dash (1981) and Black Knight (1984)?

1743.   In which year was the first Hopman Cup tennis tournament played?

1744.   Who were the two boxers who fought in a bout for the vacated heavyweight title left vacant by Joe Louis in 1949?

1745.   How many goals did Hawthorn's Peter Hudson kick in the 1970 VFL/AFL season?

1746.   What was Australian golfer Jason Day's first major championship win, achieving the feat in 2015?

1747.   Between 1921 and 1933, Benny Wearing scored 144 tries and played 172 games for which NSW rugby league club?

1748.   Which team scored the most goals at the 2014 association football World Cup?

1749.   Who made 109 appearances for Australia's Socceroos between 1993 and 2013?

1750.   The NFL team known as the Saints are located in which U.S. city?

1751.   Who was the captain of Australia's first national soccer team in 1922?

1752.   How many matches was North Melbourne (AFL) player Fred Rutley suspended for after found guilty for kicking, striking and being involved in a melee during an on field incident in a VFL match in 1925?

1753.   Why did Nigeria boycott the 1978 Commonwealth Games?

1754. Which team won the 2014 U.S. "World Series" baseball championships?

1755. The Australian Basketball League team, the Sydney Kings, were formed in 1988 with the merger of which two clubs?

1756. Who was the Adelaide player in the AFL who won the Norm Smith Medal twice; first 1997 and again 1998?

1757. What was established at Yonkers New York by Scotsman John Reid in 1888?

1758. In which year did former Collingwood full forward Brian Taylor win the Coleman Medal ?

1759. What major feat did athlete Charles Dumas achieve in 1956?

1760. Who took 10 wickets for the match during the Boxing Day test of 1981?

1761. In which year was rugby league's Canterbury-Bankstown player John Greaves first chosen to represent Australia against Great Britain?

1762. Who was the Sydney jockey who had the nicknames "Last Chance Cookie" and "The Champ"?

1763. Which country was runner-up in the Hopman Cup (tennis) in 1989 and 2003?

1764. How many times did Tony Lockett win the Coleman Medal for the highest goal scorer in an AFL season?

1765. Who was the English association footballer and manager who played 773 games for Leeds United, was capped 35 times for England and managed Middlesbrough to a second division title. He also managed Sheffield Wednesday, Newcastle United and the Republic of Ireland.

1766. Why were Carlton players Doug Fraser and Alex Lang suspended for 99 matches between 1910 and 1915?

1767. The first "Bathurst 1000" motor race, then known as the "Armstrong 500", was held at which venue?

1768. Who was the athlete who was the first to legally break the 20 second barrier for the 200 metres sprint?

1769. What was invented by Americans David Armbruster and Jack Sieg in the 1930s?

1770. Who are the only two Australian women who have won the 200 metres track gold medal at an Olympic Games?

1771. Who was the Western Australian who won North Melbourne's Syd Barker Medal in 2000?

1772. Who won the men's singles tennis title at the French Open in 2012?

1773. Who is thought to be the only VFL umpire to lose his life during fighting in World War One?

1774. In which city of the United States was softball invented in 1887?

1775. What was the original name of the Australian Basketball League team, the Townsville Crocodiles?

1776. Which sport plays for the "John Reid Shield"?

1777. Who was runner-up in the 2012 Tour de France cycle race?

1778. Who was the former Victorian state premier who became president of the Hawthorn Football Club in 2005?

1779. Who captained Western Australia's State of Origin football side in 1979, 1980 1986 and 1987?

1780. Who scored 250 during the Boxing Day cricket test of 1990?

1781. Who was the rugby league player who scored 19 points out of 22 for Eastern Suburbs against Balmain in the 1945 New South Wales rugby league grand final?

1782. Who rode the 1930 Caulfield Cup winner Amounis, the 1953 Sydney Cup winner Carioca and the 1954 CB Fisher Plate winner Rising Fast?

1783. Which team won the Hopman (tennis) Cup in 2012?

1784. Who won the AFL Coleman Medal for three years in succession; 1993, 1994 and 1995?

1785. How many times was association footballer Robbie Fowler capped for England?

1786. With which sport is Australian champion Leigh Adams associated?

1787. Where were the Winter Olympic Games held in 1988?

1788. Where will the 2018 Commonwealth Games be held?

1789. What dubious distinction does former Collingwood player Billy Pickin have as a first grade cricketer?

1790. Who was the first cricketer to score a double century in a one day international?

1791. Which AFL club awards the Carji Greeves Medal?

1792. Who was the player who won the Wally Lewis Medal in the 2008 State of Origin rugby league series?

1793. Which AFL/VFL team used Corio Oval as its home venue between 1897 and 1940?

1794. What was the record amount of goals scored by South Fremantle player Bernie Naylor in a West Australian Football League match against Subiaco in 1953?

1795. Australian Basketball League team, the Wollongong Hawks, were originally known by what other name prior to 1998?

1796. How many gold medals were won by Australia in athletics at the 2012 Paralympic Games?

1797. Which air force has an aerobatic team known as the Roulettes?

1798. Who is the woman athlete who is a holder of the women's marathon record (2011), a three time winner of the London marathon, two time winner of the New York marathon and winner of the 2002 Chicago marathon?

1799. Which three teams did England draw in the first round of the 2014 World Cup of association football?

1800. Who played his last MCG cricket test match for Australia during the Boxing Day test of 2003?

1801. Who was the rugby league player who scored the only try of the 1964 New South Wales rugby league grand final playing for St George against Balmain?

1802. Which horse, ridden by Billy Cook, defeated Phar Lap in the 1929 Chelmsford Stakes?

1803. The World Team Cup of tennis is played in which city?

1804. Which club was Roy Park playing with when he topped the goal kicking list for the VFL/AFL in 1913?

1805. How many FIFA World Cup tournaments did Diego Maradona play in during his career?

1806. Who was the jockey who rode Dunaden to victory in the 2012 Caulfield Cup?

1807. Who succeeded Hawthorn coach Ken Judge after the 1999 AFL season?

1808. Who were the two players who captained the teams in golf's 2003, 2005 and 2007 President Cup tournaments?

1809. In which country was British 5,000 and 10,000 metre Olympic gold medallist Mo Farah born?

1810. Who was the walker who was disqualified for an illegal gait as she was about to enter the stadium for the final lap during the 20km road race at the Sydney Olympic Games in 2000?

1811. Hicham El Guerrouj, a record holder for the 1,500 metres track event, is from which country?

1812. Which team was runner up to Arsenal in the 2014 FA Cup final?

1813. In which Olympiad were swimmers finally allowed to wear goggles?

1814. Which WAFL club scored a record 41 goals 30 behinds against South Fremantle in 1944?

1815. What is the name given to the New Zealand men's national basketball team?

1816. Which sport plays for the "Gilleys Shield"?

1817. Who coached West Perth in the West Australian Football League in 1982, 1983 and 1984?

1818. In which year was the Simpson Medal, an award to the best player in a WAFL grand final or state game, first presented?

1819. Where were the Winter Olympic Games held in 1952?

1820. Who was the "Man of the Match" during the Boxing Day cricket test of 2005?

1821. What position did rugby league player Brett Kenny play in for the Australian national team, New South Wales and the Parramatta Eels?

1822. Between August 28th and November 2nd 2010, which horse won the Memsie Stakes, Underwood Stakes, Yalamba Stakes, W.S. Cox Plate and the MacKinnon Stakes but ran third in the Melbourne Cup?

1823. Who was the International Tennis Federation's world men's champion in 2011?

1824. Who was the Melbourne player who kicked a record 18 goals in an VFL/AFL match against St Kilda in 1947?

1825. Who was captain of Argentina in their successful World Cup team of 1978?

1826. Who won the "Most Valued Player" award in the Trans Tasman Netball League in 2013?

1827. Who was the former Collingwood player who is/was known as the "Macedonian Marvel" or the "Magician"?

1828. What is the award given to the fairest and best player in an AFL match between Adelaide and Port Adelaide?

1829. Which Major League baseball team did Lou Gehrig play for during the 1920s and 30s?

1830. The Tampa Bay Buccaneers in the NFL are located in which state of the U.S.?

1831. Rugby league player Johnny Rapier made his first grade debut in 1957 playing for which team?

1832. Who was captain of the A-League side Newcastle Jets during the 2014-15 season?

1833. Why did thirty two nations boycott the 1986 Commonwealth Games?

1834. Name two European golfers who have won the Australian Open up to and including 2013?

1835. In how many Olympic Games did Andrew Vlahov play with the Boomers (Australian men's basketball side)?

1836. The Liffey Swim is an annual swimming race conducted in which city of the world?

1837. Which team won the World Netball Championships in 2011?

1838. Who is the Western Australian who captained Australia 28 times in cricket test matches?

1839. What is the weight of a women's shot put in open competition?

1840. Who claimed a world record of 700 wickets during the Boxing Day cricket test of 2006?

1841. Who coached the Australian rugby league "Kangaroos" to World Cup victories in 1968 and 1970?

1842. Who was the jockey who rode the winner of the W.S.Cox Plate in 1977, 1978 and 1979?

1843. Who was the International Tennis Federation's world women's champion in 2011?

1844. Who played 426 games for Hawthorn in the AFL/VFL between 1972 and 1991?

1845. For which association football national side did Gabriel Omar Batistuta score 56 goals in 78 matches?

1846. How many tries did South Sydney's Nathan Merritt score in a match against Parramatta in 2011 when they defeated that side 56-6

1847. Who became captain of the Perth Wildcats in 1993?

1848. What is the name given to the seventh hole at the Augusta National Golf Club course, home of the U.S. Masters?

1849. Who was the world heavyweight boxing champion between 1952-56 who retired after 6 successful defences of his title with a career win lose record of 49-0?

1850. How many gold medals did East German swimmer Kristin Otto win at the Seoul Olympic Games in 1988?

1851. What athletic feat was first achieved by Cuban athlete Javier Sotomayor ?

1852. Who was the former Collingwood and North Melbourne AFL player who made his American football debut with the Philadelphia Eagles in 2007 and later with the Washington Redskins in 2011?

1853. Who was the first man to run under 10 seconds for the 100 metres at low altitude and not wind assisted?

1854. Who was voted FIFA "World Footballer of the Year" in January 2015?

1855. Who was head coach of the Australian basketball team and the Adelaide 36s from 1998-2008?

1856. What is the name of the Women's Basketball League team based in Bendigo, Victoria ?

1857. Who was the first New Zealander to score a triple century in test cricket?

1858. Who received the "Golden Boot" award at the 2014 association football World Cup?

1859. Which AFL/VFL team used the Junction Oval as a venue between 1897 and 1964?

1860. Who was the "Man of the Match" during the cricket Boxing Day test of 2008?

1861. How did Australian rugby league representative John "Bomber" Peard receive his nickname of "Bomber"?

1862. In which major race did jockey Darby Munro ride the following horses to victory: Rogilla, Young Idea, Mosaic and Beau Vite?

1863. Who was the International Tennis Federation's world champion for men from 1993 to 1998?

1864. Which horse won the 2016 Perth Cup?

1865. In which city is the Italian association football team Juventus based?

1866. Who was the Melbourne Cup winning jockey who announced his retirement on 28th October 2012?

1867. Who was the Richmond player (AFL) who scored 443 goals during his career at the club?

1868. What is "The Don Award" in Australian sport?

1869. Who was the player who made 46 appearances as captain of the Socceroos between 1990 and 1996?

1870. What sport is associated with the Solheim Cup?

1871. In 1976 Cuban athlete Alberto Juantorena became the first athlete to hold titles in each of which two Olympic track events?

1872 Which sport held its world championships at Saskatoon Canada in June 2015?

1873. Who was the Australian cricketer who scored 104 in the 2013 Ryobi one day final?

1874. Who was the Collingwood player who was knocked unconscious during a behind the play incident in a match against St Kilda in July 1972. He was left in a life threatening coma for 24 hours. The incident involved a St Kilda player named Jim O'Dea.

1875. What place did the Australian men's basketball team achieve playing in their first Olympics which were held in Melbourne in 1956?

1876. At which venue did Shane Warne bowl Englishman Mike Gatting with the so called "ball of the century"?

1877. Where was Wallaby player Henry Speight born?

1878. Over what distance is the Ballarat Cup run?

1879. Who coached Richmond (AFL) for 248 games between 1966 and 1976?

1880. Who was the test cricketer who was hanged in 1955 for murdering his wife?

1881. In which year did Jack Rayner make his rugby test debut for Australia?

1882. Which horse won the W.S. Cox Plate in 2003 and 2006?

1883. Who was the International Tennis Federation's world champion for men from 2004 to 2007?

1884. Who did South African boxer Gerrie Coetzee defeat to take the WBA heavyweight title in September 1983?

1885. How old was Vic Cumberland when he played his last game for St Kilda in the VFL/AFL in 1920?

1886. In which Spanish city is the Spanish association football club RCD Espanyol located?

1887. Where were the 2014 women's world softball championships held?

1888. Which NFL team has the nicknames , the Birds , the Buzzsaw and the Cards, among others?

1889. Who coached South Australian club Norwood in 1957 and 1958 and again in 1965, 1966 and 1967?

1890. Who was voted "Man of the Match" in the first cricket test of the series played between Australia v India in 2014-15, a game played in Adelaide in December 2014?

1891. Who was the first person to break the sound barrier on land ?

1892. Who was the player who made 60 appearances as captain of Australia's Socceroos between 2006 and 2013?

1893. In which Australian city in 1900, was the first game of badminton played in Australia?

1894. Which team were world women's softball champions in 2014?

1895. Which U.S. team drafted Australian basketball player Luc Longley in 1991?

1896. Who was the player who made 60 appearances as captain of the Socceroos between 1971 and 1979?

1897. What was the name of the yacht used by Alan Bond to challenge for the 1974 America's Cup?

1898. In which city of the world is the "Cole Classic" swim race conducted?

1899. Who was captain of the A-League side Sydney FC during the 2014-15 season?

1900. Who was the test cricketer who was suspended for two months after admitting he had possessed and smoked cannabis?

1901. Who coached the rugby league team, the Parramatta Eels to three premierships, in 1981, 1982 and 1983?

1902. Who was the first female jockey to ride in the Melbourne Cup?

1903. Which U.S. doubles team were men's International Tennis Federation champions from 2003 through to 2007 and again from 2009 to 2011?

1904. Which four AFL teams did Tom Hafey coach?

1905. In which year was the association football competition known as the "A-League", founded in Australia?

1906. Who was the American cyclist who was known as "The Boss"?

1907. Which Australian football competition once included the inaugural clubs of Bankers, South Park, Prince Alfred College and Victorian?

1908. Who was captain of Germany's 2014 association football World Cup team?

1909. Which three National Ice Hockey League teams are located in the city of New York?

1910. Who captained the Hobart Hurricanes in the Big Bash League during the 2014-15 season?

1911. Who was the Australian who won the Boston marathon in 1986?

1912. Who won the Western Australian Sports Star of the Year in 2008 and 2009?

1913. Where did the first Australian national soccer team tour in 1922?

1914. Who was the Hawthorn player who, in 1972, kicked three goals with his first three kicks in the AFL/VFL ?

1915. Which two American NBA clubs did Australian basketball player Shane Heal play with?

1916. What is the name given to the fifth hole at the Augusta National Golf Club course, home of the U.S. Masters?

1917. In which year did Geelong (AFL) player Joel Selwood win a Rising Star award and also played in a premiership team?

1918. Who won the PGA championship at the Oak Hill Country Club in Rochester New York in August 2013?

1919. In which position did the West Coast Eagles finish during John Todd's two seasons as coach in 1988 and 1989?

1920. Who was the English test cricketer who spent a night in gaol after trashing his hotel room while on tour of Australia in 1994?

1921. Who were the two rugby league players who scored tries in the 1977 tied grand final between St George and Parramatta?

1922. In which year was the first radio call of the Melbourne Cup?

1923. Mary Joe Fernandez (1996), Jana Novotna (1997) and Natasha Zverva (1998), all won International Tennis Federation world women's double champion titles playing with the same American player. What was that player's name?

1924. Who was the coach of AFL club Collingwood who coached that club for a record 413 games?

1925. Which team won the title of "Champions" in the Australian "A-League" in the inaugural season of 2005-2006?

1926. In which year did Australia and Argentina first play each other in rugby union?

1927. Who was the first captain of the Perth Wildcats basketball team?

1928. Who was captain of West Perth (West Australian Football League) between 1980 and 1986?

1929. The winner of which sporting event receives the "Stonehaven Cup"?

1930. Who was the Australian athlete who won a gold medal in the women's "Road Race" and a silver medal in the 3,000 metres "Individual Pursuit" both at the Barcelona Olympic Games in 1992?

1931. In which year did Revenue win the Melbourne Cup?

1932. Which team won the 2012-13 "One Day" Australian cricket final?

1933. Who was the boxer who became the first fatality of an Australian title fight?

1934. Which NSW rugby league team won the premiership in all three grades in 1963?

1935. Who captained the Perth Wildcats in the Australian National Basketball League between 2002-2003 and 2004-2005?

1936. Which two teams played in the first Sheffield Shield cricket match which was played in December 1892?

1937. Which AFL club goes by the motto "Floreat Pica"

1938. Who were the three Australians who scored centuries in the first cricket test of the series against South Africa in February 2014?

1939. In which W.A. country town was Sydney Swans player Lance (Buddy) Franklin born?

1940. Who was the former English test cricketer who received a suspended 3 month sentence for assaulting a woman in France in 1996?

1941. Who was captain of the 1977 St George rugby league grand final side that drew with Parramatta?

1942. Who is the youngest jockey to have ridden the winner of a the Melbourne Cup?

1943. Who were the American and Australian women who won the International Tennis Federation world doubles champion title in 2005 and 2006?

1944. Who became the first heavyweight boxer to hold all three titles, WBA, WBC and the IBF at the one time?

1945. How many fairest and best awards did VFL/AFL player Bob Skelton win at South Melbourne?

1946. Which three teams were the only teams that survived the Australian National Soccer League when the competition became defunct at the end of 2003. These teams then moved to the "A League"?

1947. In which year did the horse race, "The Railway Stakes", become a Group One race?

1948. Who was the former Collingwood, Essendon and St Kilda player nicknamed "The Incredible Hulk"?

1949. Who was the player who preceded cricketer George Bailey as Australia's T-20 captain?

1950. What does the Olympic motto, "Citius, Altius Fortius" mean?

1951. Who was recognised as the 2014 men's hockey World Cup best young player?

1952. Who once said "Joe Fraser is so ugly that when he cries the tears turn around and go down the back of his head"?

1953. Who is the player who played 371 games for the West Perth Football Club in the WAFL?

1954. In which year was the VFL grand final first held at the Melbourne Cricket Ground?

1955. Who coached the Australian men's basketball in the Olympic Games from Munich in 1972 until Los Angeles in 1984?

1956. Which club did Port Adelaide play in its first match in the AFL competition in 1997?

1957. Who was the first international winner of the U.S. Masters golf tournament?

1958. In which sport did Australian Phillip Adams win 17 medals in four Commonwealth Games from 1982 to 1994?

1959. Who captained the successful South African 1995 World Cup winning rugby union team?

1960. Who was the cricket player who hit a test century at the age of 46?

1961. Who did Wayne Bennett replace as coach of the Queensland rugby league State of Origin team in 1986?

1962. Who was the first female trainer to win the Melbourne Cup/ Caulfield Cup double?

1963. The International Tennis Federation world doubles champions for 2001 were Todd Woodbridge of Australia and which other player?

1964. Who were the coach and the captain of Melbourne when they won VFL/AFL premierships in 1955, 1956, 1957, were runners-up 1958 and again premiers in 1959 and 1960?

1965. Which Australian "A-League" team played its home games at Bluetongue Stadium in Gosford?

1966. What was the name of the Australian sailor who won a gold medal in the "Laser Class" at the 2012 London Olympics?

1967. What were the racing colours of Bart Cumming's stable?

1968. Which National Ice Hockey team won the Stanley Cup in 1973-74 and 1974-75?

1969. Who was the player who received the "Golden Ball" award at the 2014 association football World Cup?

1970. Who was the athlete who was considered by Forbes to be the world's top earning athlete of 1993?

1971. What is the Phil Manassa Medal awarded for in the AFL?

1972. What feat did Australian Ken Warby achieve on the 8th of October 1978?

1973. What was the final score in the 2013 rugby league World Cup final between Australia and New Zealand?

1974. Who was the sportsman who won the "Laureus World Sportsman of the Year" award in 2012?

1975. How many Olympic Games did Australian basketball player Andrew Gaze compete at?

1976. Who was the winner of the women's singles final at the 2014 Australian tennis Open ?

1977. During which two years were the Sydney Rabbitohs excluded from the NRL competition?

1978. What was the name of the Commonwealth Games mascot for Edinburgh in 1986?

1979. Who did the Seattle Sea-Hawks defeat to win the 48th NFL Super Bowl in 2014 ?

1980. As of February 2015, who is the only cricket player to have scored a century in each innings of his 100th test?

1981. Which is the third oldest national team in rugby league?

1982. What is the name of the horse race first ran in 1867 and won by Glencoe. It is a race for two year olds run over a distance of 1,400 metres at Randwick at set weights and is part of the "Triple Crown" races which also includes the Golden Slipper and the Champagne Stakes?

1983. Who was the International Tennis Federation's champion for women's singles from 1982 until 1986?

1984. In which year did Ron Barassi leave AFL/VFL club Melbourne to take up a captain/coaching role at Carlton?

1985. Which Australian "A-League" team were premiership winners in 2010?

1986. Who won rugby union's "John Eales Medal" in 2012?

1987. At which golf course in 1974 did South African Gary Player win the Australian Open?

1988. What is the name of the trophy which has been played for in rugby union matches between Australia and Ireland since 1999?

1989. Who was the AFL player who won the aboriginal "Deadly" award for the most outstanding achievement in the AFL in 2007 and 2008?

1990. In which suburb of Sydney is the Royal Sydney Golf Club located?

1991. Where were the Winter Olympic Games held in 1960?

1992. Who was the athlete who won the gold medal for the 1,500 metres freestyle and a silver medal for the 400 metres freestyle at the Barcelona Olympics in 1992?

1993. Who was the East Perth (WAFL) player who kicked 620 goals for the club between 1962 and 1972?

1994. The Charles Sutton Medal is awarded to the fairest and best player at which AFL club?

1995. Which Australian national team is known as the Opals?

1996. Who was the former Sydney Swans player who once said, "I want to kick 70 or 80 goals this season, whichever comes first".

1997. 2014 Melbourne Cup winner Protectionist was from which country?

1998. Clive Waterhouse, number one draft choice in the 1995 AFL draft and taken by Fremantle, was recruited from which club?

1999. Who was the Australian woman athlete who broke Melinda Gainsford's 20 year 100m national record by running 11.11 seconds at the ACT championships in Canberra in February 2014?

2000. Who was the first player to take 400 wickets in both test and one day internationals?

2001. Which team, in 1935, became the first European champions in rugby league?

2002. Which horse race was once known as the Caulfield Stakes prior to 1997. It is a race for three year olds and upwards, a weight for age race run over 2,000 metres at Caulfield racecourse. It was inaugurated in 1886. Past winners include: Rising Fast (1954), Kingston Town (1981-82), Bonecrusher (1986) Might and Power (1998) and Northerly (2001)?

2003. How many times was Steffi Graf International Tennis Federation's women's singles champion?

2004. Who did John Northey replace as coach of AFL/VFL club Melbourne in 1986?

2005. Which Australian "A-League" team won the premiership and the champions title in both 2006-2007 and 2008-2009?

2006. Which three clubs did AFL player Dermott Brereton play with between 1982 and 1995?

2007. What are the four divisions of the National Hockey League of North America?

2008. Which team won the 2013/14 Australian baseball championships in February 2014 ?

2009. In which year was the horse race, "The Railway Stakes" first run?

2010. Who was the boxer who knocked out heavyweight champion Mike Tyson in a bout in Tokyo in February 1990?

2011. Which club did Wallaby Adam Ashley-Cooper make his Super Rugby debut with in 2005?

2012. Who was the high profile English player who joined the Newcastle Jets in the Australian A-League in 2012?

2013. Who was the driver who won the 2013 Indian Formula One Grand Prix?

2014. Where was Australian Wallaby, Clyde Rathbone born?

2015. Which WNBA team drafted Australian woman basketball player Lauren Jackson in 2001?

2016. In which year did Footscray (Western Bulldogs) player Gary Dempsey win the Brownlow Medal?

2017. How many tries did West Tigers player Lote Turqiri score in the 2010 season?

2018. Which Scottish association football club plays its home games Tulloch Caledonian stadium?

2019.   Who won the 2014 AFL Brownlow Medal?

2020.   Up to 2015, who was the only bowler to have taken 40 wickets in a cricket test series twice?

2021.   Who became European champions of rugby league in 1938-39?

2022.   What is the name of the Group One race which was inaugurated in 1897, is now run over 1,600 metres (was 1,400), a weight for age race ran at Caulfield with past winners including Manikato (1979, 1980, 1981), Gunsynd (1972), Ajax (1938, 1939, 1940), Phar Lap (1930), Bernborough (1946) and 2011 winner More Joyous?

2023.   How many times was Australian Lleyton Hewitt International Tennis Federation world men's singles champion?

2024.   Who did AFL club Hawthorn defeat with a kick after the siren to win the 1987 preliminary final?

2025.   Who did the Newcastle Jets (Australian "A- League") defeat to win the Champion's title in 2007-2008 season?

2026.   Who skippered the Australian yacht "Southern Cross" in the 1974 America's Cup challenge?

2027.   Who was runner-up to Rafael Nadal in the men's singles at the 2013 French tennis Open?

2028.   Who was awarded the 2014 "Joyce Brown Netball Coach of the Year"?

2029.   Which team did Nicole Bolton play with in the Australian Women's National Cricket League during 2014-15?

2030. Which National Ice Hockey League team has a penguin as its symbol?

2031. Name the Hawthorn player and Peter Crimmins Medal winner who played 189 consecutive games for the club?

2032. Who captained the Brisbane Heat in the Big Bash League during the 2014-15 season?

2033. In which event did Australian Sally Pearson win an Olympic gold medal at the 2012 London Olympic Games?

2034. Who was the player who received the "Golden Glove" award for the 2014 association football World Cup?

2035. In which year was the Australian Women's National Basketball League founded?

2036. Who was the coach of East Perth (WAFL) between 1956 and 1964 and again in 1969?

2037. What is the name of the Women's Basketball League team based in Canberra in 2015?

2038. Who rode the winner of the 2014 "Magic Millions" , a horse race run on the Gold Coast in Queensland ?

2039. Who was crickets "Man of the Test Series" between Australia and South Africa played in early 2014?

2040. How many consecutive tests matches did Australian cricketer Allan Border play?

2041. In which year was the "World Sevens" rugby league competition introduced?

2042. Which South Australian Group One race run over 1,200 metres was won by Takeover Target in 2009 and Lone Rock in 2011? Prior to 2007 it had been a handicap race.

2043. In which year was American Jim Courier International Tennis Federation's men's singles champion?

2044. Who replaced John Northey as coach of Melbourne at the end of the 1992 AFL season?

2045. What was the record unbeaten run of matches recorded by Brisbane Roar in the Australian A-League competition?

2046. What is the name given to the three person keel boat that is used in open competition in the Paralympic Games?

2047. Who was considered by Forbes to be the world's top earning athlete of 1997?

2048. Which two NFL teams are located in the state of Missouri?

2049. The Gordon Willoughby Medal is awarded to the player of the year by members of which NRL club?

2050. What was the former name of the New York Yankees before it was changed in 1913?

2051. Who was German association football World Cup coach in 2014?

2052. How many games did Jack Dyer play for the Richmond Football Club (VFL/AFL)?

2053. In which year did record game holder Michael Tuck make his AFL/VFL debut?

2054. Which club did South Adelaide score a record 39 goals 16 points against in a match at Football Park in 1984?

2055. As of 2015, how many times have the Adelaide Lightning won the Australian Women's National Basketball League championship?

2056. In which year was the first Bathurst 1000 (then known as the Armstrong 500) held?

2057. Which two Australian clubs did basketball player Carl Bruton play for before he joined the Perth Wildcats in 1987?

2058. What was test cricketer Colin Milburn's highest score for Western Australia in a Sheffield Shield match?

2059. What is the Espirito Santo Trophy awarded for?

2060. What do the following test cricketers have in common? Amir Elahi, Gul Mohammad and A.H. Kardar.

2061. Who won the "World Sevens" rugby plate in 1992?

2062. What is the name of the first leg of the autumn sprint series in the Melbourne carnival? A race ran over 1000m at Flemington in February. The other two legs being the Oakleigh Plate (1100 metres) and the Newmarket Handicap (1200 metres)?

2063. In which year was American Andy Roddick International Tennis Federation's men's single champion?

2064. Who took over as coach of AFL side Melbourne in 1998?

2065. In which year did Gold Coast United enter the Australian association football "A-League" competition?

2066. How many seasons did Jack Oatey coach the Sturt Football Club in the SANFL?

2067. What is the weight of a discus used in men's open competition?

2068. Who is the boxer known as "Dr Steelhammer"?

2069. Which team won the first women's world softball championships held in Melbourne in 1965?

2070. Which American National Ice Hockey team won the Stanley Cup in 2011?

2071. Which Scottish association football club based in Leith north of Edinburgh are sometimes referred to as "The Cabbage"?

2072. What is the name of the annual award given to the club champion at the AFL's Brisbane Lions?

2073. What was the Graham Moss Medal awarded for?

2074. What is the name of the netball team out of Perth Western Australia that play in the Trans Tasman Netball League?

2075. In which year did the Australian Institute of Sport's women's basketball team win the WNBL championship?

2076. What was the object or trophy given to the winner of the first Melbourne Cup?

2077. Who was considered by Forbes to be the world's top earning athlete of 2006?

2078. In which sport is Melissa Wu an Australian champion and Olympic silver medallist?

2079. Who was the golfer who won the 2012 British Open?

2080. What major feat was achieved by test cricketer Hasan Raza of Pakistan?

2081. In which year was the Super League "World Nines" rugby league competition introduced?

2082. The Global Sprint Challenge is a series of 10 thoroughbred races ran in which six countries as of 2012?

2083. Who won the 2016 Australian Open men's singles tennis final?

2084. Who was captain of AFL club Melbourne from 1991 until 1997?

2085. In which season did Melbourne Heart play its first "A -League" game?

2086. Who was the player who won the Wally Lewis Medal for the 2004 State of Origin rugby league series?

2087. Which team won cricket's 2013/14 Sheffield Shield?

2088. Who was the Australian test cricketer who scored 151 on his test debut playing against India in 2004?

2089. Who did the Brisbane Bears defeat to win their first game in the AFL?

2090. Who was the jockey who had his 100th Group One win on Derby Day 2013?

2091. Who was captain of the A-League side Wellington Phoenix during the 2014-15 season?

2092. What was the worst placed seasonal position of the West Coast Eagles under coach Mick Malthouse?

2093. Who was the inaugural winner of rugby union's John Eales Medal?

2094. Who won the Laureus World Sports award for men in 2001?

2095. In which year did the Australian WNBL team, the Bendigo Spirit , join the competition?

2096. Who defeated the world heavyweight title holder Buster Douglas at Douglas' first defence of his title in October 1990?

2097. Which state did former AFL star Jason Dunstall originate from?

2098. Who was the rider who won the 2012 Spanish MotoGP?

2099. Who did Andy Murray defeat to win the 2013 Wimbledon men's singles tennis final?

2100. Which two countries played the first international cricket match?

2101. Which three countries each won rugby league's "World Nines" trophy, plate and bowl in 1997?

2102. Which horse won the Linlithgow Stakes/The Age Classic (now known as the Patinack Farm Classic) for three years in succession in 1931, 1932 and 1933?

2103. Who was the woman tennis player who recorded a tennis serve of 205 km/h?

2104. Which VFL/AFL club was the first to win three premierships in a row?

2105. Which club did Wellington Phoenix replace in the Australian "A-League" competition?

2106. Who was the former Australian test cricketer who coached Zimbabwe between 2001 and 2004 and later Sri Lanka between 2011 and 2012?

2107. What feat did American Major League baseball player Jackie Robinson achieve in April 1947?

2108. How many appearances did John Kosmina make with the Socceroos as captain?

2109. How old was Indian cricketer Sachin Tendulkar when he made his test debut?

2110. The NFL Seahawks are located in which U.S. city?

2111. Boxer Anthony Mundine played rugby league for which three NRL clubs?

2112. Who was the inaugural captain of the Brisbane Bears in the VFL /AFL?

2113. Which four London association football clubs play the West London derbies?

2114. How many times did Sydney Swan, Barry Hall, top the club's goal kicking list?

2115. Which team were champions in the Australian Women's National Basketball League in 2011?

2116. Which NBL team did Tom Jervis play with during the 2014-15 season?

2117. Who was the West Coast Eagles player who won "Mark of the Year" in 2004?

2118. Who was the former AFL/VFL player who was known as "The Chimp"?

2119. How old was racehorse Vintage Crop when it died?

2120. When was the first all England cricket XI formed?

2121. How many times has rugby league player Andrew Johns (NSW) been "Man of the Match" in State of Origin games?

2122. What was New Zealand born racehorse Phar Lap's final race?

2123. Who was the first tennis player to wear shorts at Wimbledon?

2124. Who was the player who captained AFL club Carlton to three premierships and replaced Ron Barassi, becoming captain coach of that club ?

2125. Which Australian "A-League" club closed in March 2011 due to financial problems?

2126. Which association football club won the first Club World Cup (Championship) which was held in Brazil in 2000?

2127. What nickname did WAFL club Subiaco have prior to 1973?

2128. Which winter sport was invented in medieval Scotland and involved the use of a large polished stone?

2129. Which yacht was declared overall winner of the 2013 Sydney to Hobart yacht race?

2130. Who was the first Carlton player to kick 100 goals in a season?

2131. What is a Cibi?

2132. How many appearances did Mark Viduka make with the Socceroos as captain?

2133. Which team, along with the Vancouver Canucks, joined the American National Ice Hockey League in 1970-71 season. Their home arena is known as the First Niagara Center.

2134. Who was the Australian test cricketer who scored 165 not out on his test debut for Australia playing against England at the Melbourne Cricket Ground in 1876-77?

2135. Which Australian Women's National Basketball team won the championship in 2000, 2002, 2003, 2006, 2007, 2009 and 2010?

2136. Who did Novak Djokovic play in the final of the men's singles tennis at the 2016 Australian Open?

2137. Which team won the 2014 Australian National Rugby League premiership?

2138. What is name of the annual major marathon which is run between Newcastle-Upon-Tyne and South Shields in England?

2139. Which English Premier League team was managed by Arsene Wenger during 2014-15?

2140. What Australian cricket team visited England in 1868?

2141. How many times was rugby league player Wally Lewis "Man of the Match" in State of Origin games?

2142. Near which town in New Zealand was racehorse Phar Lap born in 1926?

2143. What type of sporting club were the first U.S. National Tennis Championships for women played at in 1887?

2144. What number jersey was worn by Carlton great, Alex Jesaulenko?

2145. Who was the former East German national coach who was associated with Perth Glory in the Australian National Soccer League from 1999 until 2001 ?

2146. What is the name of the medal awarded in the AFL for "Mark of the Year"?

2147. In which year did Shane Warne of Australia bowl Mike Gatting of England with the so called "ball of the century"?

2148. What do the following Melbourne Cup winners have in common: Wotan, Old Rowley and The Pearl?

2149. Who coached the Sydney Sixers in the Big Bash League during the 2014-15 season?

2150. Who won the 2013 Japanese Formula One Grand Prix?

2151. Who was named "Man of the Match" after the second Ashes test in Adelaide in December 2013?

2152. In which state was Australian test fast bowler Mitchell Johnson born?

2153. Who was the winner of the 2014 Tour Down Under cycling event?

2154. Which horse was placed second for the third time in a Melbourne Cup following the 2014 race?

2155. Which Australian Women's National Basketball team were champions in 2004 and 2005?

2156. Who was the rugby union player who won the John Eales Medal in 2014?

2157. Which three English county cricket sides did Australian Michael Hussey play with?

2158. What are the six nations that have attended every Commonwealth/Empire Games?

2159. Who won the men's Quiksilver Pro surfing event on the Gold Coast in March 2014?

2160. What was the nickname given to Australian test cricketer Fred Spofforth?

2161. How many times was rugby league player Peter Sterling "Man of the Match" in State of Origin games?

2162. Which horse sired the racehorse Phar Lap?

2163. Who was the male tennis player who recorded a serve of 251 km/h during a Davis Cup tie in 2011?

2164. How many times did heavyweight boxing champion of the world Rocky Marciano defend his title?

2165. Who coached AFL club Carlton from 1981 to 1985?

2166. In which year did the predecessor of the "A-League" in Australia, the National Soccer League, come into existence?

2167. What is the hometown of Australian professional surfer Joel Parkinson?

2168. Which team did Australian Adam Gilchrist play for in the Indian Premier League in 2011?

2169. Which VFL/AFL team scored their lowest score for a match (8 points) in a game against St Kilda in 1961?

2170. What colour dot on a squash ball indicates that the ball has a speed which is fast and a bounce which is very high?

2171. Which English Premier League team was managed by Sam Allardyce in 2014-15?

2172. In which year was the London marathon first run?

2173. Who were the two Australian batsmen who scored centuries in the first Ashes test at the Gabba in November 2013?

2174. What type sport involves a competition known as a "Puissance"?

2175. The Logan Thunder compete in which sporting competition in Australia?

2176. Who is the Queenslander and cricketer who made 119 test appearances for Australia between 1988 and 1999 during which time he scored 4,356 runs?

2177. Who was captain of the A-League side Perth Glory during the 2014-15 season?

2178. In which year did Grand Flaneur win the Melbourne Cup?

2179. Which team won FIFA Confederations Cup in 1997, 2005, 2009 and 2013?

2180. Who was the captain of the Australian cricket team during the English/Australian test match of 1882?

2181. How many times did Bill Harrigan referee rugby league State of Origin matches between 1991 and 2003?

2182. Which Group One race is the first leg of the Sydney 3year old "Triple Crown"? The other legs being the Rosehill Guineas (2000) and the AJC Derby (2400)

2183. What was unusual about the first round tennis match at Wimbledon between John Isner and Nicolas Mahut in 2010?

2184. Who captained AFL club Carlton from 1987 until 1997?

2185. Which club won the last two titles of the now defunct Australian National Soccer League (NSL)?

2186. Who coached the SANFL's Norwood Football Club between 1980 and 1990?

2187. Which overseas clubs had Harry Kewell played with before returning to Australia to play with Melbourne Victory,

2188. After which international was Australian Socceroo coach Holger Osieck sacked in 2013 for losing 6-0

2189. What is the colour of the jersey awarded to the winner of the cycling race known as "The Tour Down Under"?

2190. How many medals were won by Finnish athlete Paavo Nurmi during his Olympic career which included the 1920, 1924 and 1928 Olympic Games?

2191. Who was the player who played 355 games for the Brisbane Broncos between 1995 and 2011?

2192. Where were the Winter Olympics held in 1928?

2193. In which year did rugby union's Phil Waugh win the John Eales Medal?

2194. Which English association football club are known as the Royals?

2195. The Sydney Flames compete in which sporting competition in Australia?

2196. Who was the player who hit a record fast century off 39 balls in an Australian Big Bash match in January 2014?

2197. What is the name of the golf club located at South Oakleigh in Victoria which has been a venue for the Australian Open, Australian Women's Open and the Victorian Open?

2198. What was the name of the Commonwealth Games mascot in Auckland in 1990?

2199. Who won the 2013 "Bathurst 1000" motor race?

2200. Who was the Australian test cricketer who scored 188 in an Ashes test match, it being his maiden century and an innings which at the time,was the highest score by a player under twenty one in an Ashes series?

2201. How old was Queensland rugby league player Ben Ikin when he first played State of Origin?

2202. Who trained the racehorse Vo Rogue?

2203. What was the nickname given to the former number one American tennis player Helen Willis Moody?

2204. Who was the person who replaced Wayne Brittan as coach of AFL club Carlton at the end of the 2002 season?

2205. Who was the German association footballer who won "Footballer of the Year" in 1972 and 1976?

2206. How many players can be ready to take the field (On the sidelines dress and ready) in an American NFL game?

2207. What sporting first was achieved by a Mrs E. Widdis of Gippsland, Victoria in November 1915?

2208. Who was the Major League baseball player who played for the New York Yankees and was also married to American actress Marilyn Monroe?

2209. Who did Sam Stosur of Australia defeat to win the final of the 2014 Japanese Tennis Open?

2210. As of 2015, which American National Ice Hockey League team had won 24 Stanley Cups?

2211. Which club won the FIFA Club World Cup in 2013?

2212. Who was the person who led the 1988 New Zealand challenge for the America's Cup yacht race?

2213. How old was the horse Catalogue when it won the 1938 Melbourne Cup?

2214. What is the name given to the sixteenth hole at the Augusta National Golf Club course, home of the U.S. Masters?

2215. The Townsville Fire compete in which Australian sporting competition?

2216. Who was the Perth Wildcat basketball player who played with the Atlanta Hawks in 1993?

2217. Who partnered racing driver Peter Brock in his "Hardie Ferodo 1000" wins at Mount Panorama in 1978, 1979 and 1980?

2218. Who was the Australian cricketer who scored 117 on his Australian test debut playing against South Africa in 2008-2009?

2219. Which nation won the men's 4 x 100m swimming freestyle relay at the London Olympic Games in 2012?

2220. In which town was test cricketer Don Bradman born?

2221. How many goals were scored by rugby league player Ryan Girdler for New South Wales during the 2000 series of State of Origin?

2222. Who rode racehorse Vo Rogue for 22 of his 26 wins?

2223. How old was Martina Hingus when she was ranked number one woman tennis player in the world in 1997?

2224. Who was the player who played 375 league games for AFL club Carlton between 1986 and 2002?

2225. As of 2015 which club had won the association football's European Cup 10 times?

2226. In which year did Australia first win the Davis Cup tennis tournament?

2227. Who is the Western Australian who made 7,696 runs in test cricket for Australia?

2228. In which sport did Pakistani Janshar Khan win eight British Open titles?

2229. How many points did Wallaby Stirling Mortlock score in a match against South Africa at Docklands in Melbourne in 2000?

2230. Which team finished second in the medal count at the 1928 Amsterdam Olympic Games ?

2231. Who was the Western Bulldogs player who once said, " I've never had major knee surgery on any other part of my body."

2232. What world boxing title was won by Albert Griffiths in September 1890, making it the first world boxing title won by an Australian?

2233. Who is the Queenslander and former Australian test cricketer who made 38 test appearances between 1995 and 2006, taking 113 wickets and making 445 runs?

2234. Who was the former Sheffield Shield cricketer who won the Simpson Medal for the best player in the 1972 West Australian Football League grand final?

2235. The Australian Women's Basketball League team, the West Coast Waves, were previously known by which two other names?

2236. Who was the Australian netball player who was named "Australia's Most Valued Player" in 1996, 1998, 2002 and 2006?

2237. What were the bowling figures of Australian fast bowler Mitchell Johnson in the second innings of the second Ashes test against England at the Adelaide Oval in December 2013?

2238. What trophy was the following team of golfers runners-up to in 1998: Kim Fenton, Brett Rumford, Aaron Baddeley and Brendon Jones?

2239. Who claimed the world heavyweight boxing title at his fifth attempt when he defeated Ezzard Charles in July 1951?

2240. How many first class centuries did cricketer Don Bradman score?

2241. How many tries were scored by rugby league player Loti Tuqiri for Queensland during the 2000 State of Origin series?

2242. Which horse won the Melbourne Cup in 1950 carrying 59.5 kg (9st 5lbs)?

2243. Where in the United States is the International Tennis Hall of Fame located?

2244. Which grand final in the AFL/VFL saw a record crowd of 121,696 attend?

2245. Which association football club was European Cup champions in 1973-74, 1974-75, and 1975-76?

2246. In which year was netball first introduced into the Commonwealth Games?

2247. Who is the Australian association footballer who has played with the following clubs: Millwall (1995 2001), Blackburn Rovers (2001-2007), West Ham United (2007-2009), Everton (2009-2010) , Galatasaray (2010-2011) and Al Jazia (as of 2012)

2248. What position did the West Coast Eagles finish in their first year of competition under coach Ron Alexander?

2249. Who rode the 2013 Victoria Derby winner Polanski?

2250. Which English association football club are known as "The Blades"?

2251. What feat was achieved by swimmers Dorothy Davenport-Hill, Sarah "Fanny" Durak and Mina Wiley in April 1909?

2252. What is the name of the only non Victorian club to have competed in the Victorian Football League, a side that entered the competition in 2001 but was withdrawn in 2008?

2253. Which team won the FINA World Cup of women's water polo in 2006?

2254. In which year did rugby union's David Lyons win the John Eales Medal?

2255. Which team did the following Australian players all play for in the U.S. Women's National Basketball Association: Michele Timms, Penny Taylor, Belinda Snell, Kristi Harrower, Trisha Fallon and Michelle Brogan?

2256. In which year did David Beckham transfer to Spanish club Real Madrid?

2257. Which horse won the 2014 Perth Cup?

2258. Who won the 2014 Clive Churchill Medal?

2259. Who was the Australian flag bearer at the opening ceremony of the 2014 Glasgow Commonwealth Games?

2260. Who was captain of the English cricket team during the "Bodyline" series of 1932-33?

2261. How many points were scored by rugby league player Ryan Girdler for New South Wales during the 2000 State of Origin series?

2262. Who rode Rocket Racer to the controversial 1987 Perth Cup win?

2263. How old was tennis player Ken Rosewall when he won the Australian Open in 1972?

2264. What do the following AFL Norm Smith Medallists have in common? Chris Judd, Maurice Rioli, Gary Ablett Sr and Nathan Buckley?

2265. Who did Scottish side Celtic defeat to win the 1966-67 European Cup?

2266. Which cricket team won the 2014 men's world T20 final?

2267. What was the name of the jockey that rode the 2014 Grand National winner Pineau De Re?

2268. Who was the first Australian to score a century on debut in a one day cricket international?

2269. Which horse won the Winterbottom Stakes at Ascot racecourse in Perth in 2013?

2270. For how many seasons did John Worsfold coach the AFL's West Coast Eagles?

2271. What event awards the "Commissioner Trophy" to the winner?

2272. Who is the Australian female boxer who won a world WBC super featherweight and a world WIBA super featherweight title in 2013-2014 and 2011-12 ?

2273. As a member of the north/east division in the Eastern Conference of the National Ice Hockey League, which team plays it home games at Scotiabank Place ?

2274. Which country won the Davis Cup (tennis) for seven years in a row from 1920-26?

2275. Which three Australian clubs did basketball player James Crawford play with?

2276. Who was the Hawthorn (AFL) player who kicked 915 goals during his career?

2277. What international feat was achieved by the following team of people in July 2014: Cate Campbell, Bronte Campbell, Emma McKeon and Melanie Schlanger?

2278.	Which Big Bash team did the following players play with during the 2014-15 Big Bash season: Daniel Vettori, Andrew Flintoff and Samuel Badree?

2279.	Who was the boxer who defeated Cuban Jose Legra at London's Albert Hall on January 21st 1969 to became the WBC featherweight champion of the world?

2280.	Who was the Australian batsman who received a blow to the head while batting in the 3rd test in Adelaide during the "Bodyline" series of 1932-33?

2281.	How many consecutive appearances did rugby league player Gary Larson make for Queensland in State of Origin matches between 1991 and 1998?

2282.	Which horse, ridden by Neville Sellwood, won the Golden Slipper Stakes in 1957?

2283.	How many times has Andre Agassi won the men's singles title at the Australian Open tennis tournament?

2284.	Who were the two players who drew for the Norm Smith Medal in the 2010 AFL grand final?

2285.	In which city is the cycling event known as the "Tour Down Under" held?

2286.	Who was the first Australian to score a goal in an association football World Cup qualifying match?

2287.	What is the weight division in boxing where participants weigh between 79.4 kg and 90.7kg?

2288. On what day was the horse race, "The Railway Stakes" run prior to 2001 after which the West Australian Turf Club rescheduled the race to late November?

2289. In which English city is the cricket test venue of Headingley?

2290. Who was 2011 Australian Institute of Sport "Athlete of the Year"?

2291. In which two events did Australian athlete Jane Fleming win gold medals at the 1990 Auckland Commonwealth Games?

2292. Who are the only two Australian boxers who have been inducted into the modern era boxing Hall of Fame?

2293. How many players of a netball team are allowed on the court at one time?

2294. Which two teams played off in the final of the 1997 FIFA Confederation Cup?

2295. Which two Australian basketball clubs did Leroy Logins play with between 1981 and 2001?

2296. What is a "bascule" as described in the sport of show jumping?

2297. What is the name of the netball team out of Invercargill New Zealand that plays in the Trans Tasman Netball League?

2298. How many games did Kevin Bartlett play with Richmond Football Club in the VFL/AFL?

2299. Who was the 2014 MotoGP world champion?

2300. In which year was the first women's cricket test played?

2301. How many times did rugby league player Andrew Ettingshausen represent New South Wales in State of Origin?

2302. How many races did the racehorse Gunsynd win in his career?

2303. Who were the tennis doubles pair who won 12 Grand Slam doubles between 1965 and 1976?

2304. What was world heavyweight boxing champion Joe Louis' full name?

2305, Essendon (AFL) coach, John Worsfold once played with which WAFL club?

2306. Who was the manager of the Socceroo's team that made the 1974 association football World Cup finals?

2307. What is the sport of futsal?

2308. Who was coach of the A-League side Wellington Phoenix during the 2014-15 season?

2309. Who was the golfer who won the 2012 Australian Open?

2310. What is the name given to the eighth hole at the Augusta National Golf Club course, home of the U.S. Masters?

2311. What was the name of the Olympic Games mascot in Moscow in 1980?

2312. Who was the test cricketer who scored four double centuries in a calender year in 2012?

2313. What is the name given to the seventeenth hole at the Augusta National Golf Club course, home of the U.S. masters?

2314. In which year did Australian golfer Aaron Baddeley turn professional?

2315. With which club did former Australian basketball player Carl Bruton play his first game in the NBL in 1979?

2316. Who was the driver who won the Bahrain Formula One Grand Prix in April 2014?

2317. How many times did Phil Matera top the West Coast Eagles (AFL) goal kicking?

2318. Who was the last player to win the Graham Moss Medal which was awarded in 1998?

2319. Who was the rugby union player who won the John Eales Medal in 2005?

2320. What was the nickname given to Australian all round cricketer Keith Miller?

2321. How many goals did rugby league player Mal Meninga score for Queensland in State of Origin matches?

2322. How many successive wins were achieved by the horse Gloaming?

2323. Who were the women's doubles pair who won 20 Grand Slam tournaments between 1981 and 1989?

2324. Who was the Australian boxing champion who died in America in 1917?

2325. What was the home ground of the VFL's South Melbourne Football Club in Melbourne?

2326. Who was the manager of the 1998 Australian Socceroos association football World Cup campaign?

2327. How many Olympic gold medals did Australian swimmer Ian Thorpe win in his career?

2328. Who was considered by Forbes to be the world's top earning athlete of 2003?

2329. In which event did Michael Shelley win a gold medal at the 2014 Commonwealth Games?

2330. Which is the only English association football club which has a day of the week in their name?

2331. Which Formula One Grand Prix did Australian Daniel Riccardo win in July 2014?

2332. Which NHL team won the Stanley Cup in 2015?

2333. Who did Mexico defeat 2-1 to win its first Olympic football title during the 2012 Olympic Games?

2334. Which team did Marc Marquez represent as winner of the 2014 MotoGP Championship?

2335. Which team did American/Australian basketball player
Scott Fisher begin his NBL career with in 1987?

2336. Who won the 2012 Australian MotoGP?

2337. In which event did Royal family member Zara Phillips win a
silver medal at the 2012 London Olympic Games?

2338 Who captained Western Australia's first State of Origin
football side in 1977?

2339. Who was the Australian "A"-League player who won the
Johnny Warren Medal in 2010-11?

2340. Which Australian Football League (Victorian Football League)
club did test cricketer Keith Miller play with?

2341. How many tries did rugby league player Dale Shearer score for
Queensland in State of Origin matches?

2342. Which horse won the Sydney Cup in 1921 and the Caulfield
Cup in 1920. A horse which at 4 years old won 12 of his 13
starts.

2343. How long did it take Steffi Graf to defeat Natasha Zvereva in
the 1988 women's singles final at the French Open?

2344. What was the name given to the 1945 AFL/VFL grand final
between Carlton and South Melbourne because of the violent
nature of the game that was played?

2345. What was the record score in the association football World
Cup qualifying match between Australia and American Samoa
in 2002?

2346. Who won the men's singles final of the Brazil Open tennis tournament in February 2013?

2347. Which air force has an aerobatic team known as the "Silver Falcons"?

2348. Who was the Australian batsman who scored 201 not out as a "nightwatchman" in a test match in 2006?

2349. In which year did Cristiano Ronaldo transfer from Manchester United to Real Madrid?

2350. As of 2015, which American National Ice Hockey League team has not won a Stanley Cup since 1967?

2351. What is the name of the companion event to the cycling race known as "The Tour Down Under"?

2352. What score did Australian cricketer Bill Ponsford make on his test debut against England in 1924-25?

2353. Which AFL/VFL teams did the father of former Brisbane Lion player, Jonathan Brown, Brian Brown, play with in the 1970s and 1980s?

2354. Who was the Australian heavyweight boxer who challenged for the world heavyweight title against Vladimir Klischkov in April 2014?

2355. Who replaced Carl Bruton as coach of the Perth Wildcats (NBL) in 1989?

2356. Who was the Western Australian trainer who won nine races with Miss Andretti before he sold a 75% share of the horse to Sean Buckley and Gabriella Guenzi with the horse later trained by Lee Freedman?

2357. As of 2015, how many times has golfer Karrie Webb won the Australian Ladies Masters?

2358. What was the name of the yacht that took line honours in the Sydney to Hobart yacht race in 2005, 2006, 2007, 2008 and 2010, also taking handicap honours in 2005 and setting a new record.

2359. Who was the jockey that rode Dear Demi to victory in the 2012 Crown Oaks at Flemington?

2360. Which country won cricket's first "World Cup" in 1975?

2361. How many points did rugby league player Mal Meninga score in State of Origin matches?

2362. Which Australian horse won the Japan Cup in 1990?

2363. Who won the first singles Wimbledon tennis championship in 1877?

2364. Who became heavyweight boxing champion of the world by defeating Max Baer at Madison Square Garden, New York in June 1935?

2365. As of 2015, which is the only AFL team to have scored over two hundred points in successive matches?

2366. Who was the player who kicked the deciding goal in the penalty shoot out against Uruguay in Sydney to advance Australia into the 2006 association football World Cup finals in Germany?

2367. In which sporting event did Laura Peel of Australia win a silver medal during a World Cup tournament in February 2013?

2368. Which horse won the 1934 Melbourne Cup?

2369. Which team won the gold medal for the men's hockey at the 2012 London Olympic Games?

2370. Who was the winner of the 1987 MotoGP championship, riding for Honda?

2371. Which English club did South Sydney player Sam Burgess play with before joining the Australian club in 2010 season?

2372. Who won the 2014 Margaret River Men's Surfing Pro?

2373. Which city do the Deccan Chargers in cricket's Indian Premier League, represent?

2374. Who was the player who topped the West Coast Eagles (AFL) goal kicking in 2001?

2375. Who was the first captain of the Australian National Basketball League club, the Perth Wild Cats, appointed in 1982?

2376. Who won the Laureus World Sportswomen award for 2014?

2377. What event in the Winter Olympic Games requires a competitor to slide down an iced track on a sled, face up?

2378. Who was the English batsman who became the first "caught Marsh bowled Lillee" victim?

2379. Who was the jockey who rode the winner of the 2012 Melbourne Cup?

2380. Which country was runner up to Australia in the 1999 cricket World Cup ?

2381. Who was runner-up to Great Britain in the 1954 rugby league World Cup?

2382. What well known racehorse of the late nineteenth and early twentieth century was nicknamed "Old Jack"?

2383. In which year did women's singles and men's doubles tennis events begin at Wimbledon?

2384. Who was the Australian WBA light middleweight, WBA Super middleweight and IBO middleweight champion boxer who also played State of Origin rugby league football?

2385. In which year did the Sydney Swans make its first grand final appearance since the club relocated from Melbourne, known then as South Melbourne?

2386. Who won the 2015 Australian Ladies Masters golf tournament?

2387. Who was the American Major League baseball player who was nicknamed the "Commerce Comet"?

2388. Who succeeded Barry Davis as coach of Essendon (AFL) in 1981?

2389. How many points did Wallaby James O'Conner score in a match against France at Stad de France in Saint Denis in 2010?

2390. What sporting feat was achieved by Englishman Allan Steel in 1884?

2391. What 260 year tradition was broken by the Royal and Ancient Club of St Andrews in September 2014?

2392. What is the nickname of the Australian Hockey League women's team from Western Australia?

2393. Olympian Birgit Fischer of Germany won eight gold medals and four silver at the Olympics between 1980 and 2004 while participating in which sport?

2394. Who was the Australian player who scored a hat trick of goals in the men's world hockey cup final in 2014?

2395. Who was the coach of the Boomers (Australian men's basketball team) at the 1988 and 1992 Olympic Games?

2396. Who was the rugby union player who won the John Eales Medal in 2006?

2397. Who was considered by Forbes to be the world's top earning athlete of 2008?

2398. What event was held between NSW and Queensland in Sydney for the first time in August 1882?

2399. Who were the first pair of twins to play 100 AFL games?

2400. Who was the bowler who took 19 wickets in the 4th Ashes test match at Old Trafford in 1956?

2401. What is the nickname of the national Argentinian rugby league team?

2402. Which horse carried 10st 4lb on a heavy track to win the 1934 Doomben Handicap?

2403. How old was Charlotte Dod when she won a Wimbledon women's singles event in 1887?

2404. Who was the coach of the VFL/AFL Swans in 1982, the year they relocated to Sydney?

2405. Who did Socceroo Lucas Neill bring down in the penalty area against Italy in the 2006 association football World Cup match that allowed Italy to score and deny Australia a place in the last eight?

2406. What was the name of the horse that carried 66kg while running in the 1890 Melbourne Cup?

2407. As of 2015, how many times has Premier League club Arsenal been runners-up in the FA Cup?

2408. Who was the Brisbane Bronco player who scored 3 tries and 7 goals in a match against the Northern Eagles at ANZ stadium in May 2002?

2409. Who was the former AFL coach who once said, "Don't think, Do"?

2410. Which American National Ice Hockey team is based in Raleigh North Carolina?

2411. Who won the MotoGP championship from 1994-98?

2412. Which two countries played the first women's cricket test match?

2413. In 1883, Bobby Kinnear became the first aboriginal to achieve what sporting feat?

2414. Who was the golf associate Tiger Woods split with in 2014?

2415. Who was head coach of the Australian NBL Townsville Crocodiles from 2006 until 2011?

2416. Who became world heavyweight boxing champion on June 14th 1934 by knocking out Italian title holder Primo Carnera?

2417. Who was the Wallaby player who became captain of the Australian side at the age of 23 years and 70 days in 1982?

2418. Who was the Geelong (AFL) player who missed the team bus before the VFL/AFL Preliminary Final against Collingwood in 1981 and was replaced in the team by Peter Johnston.

2419. Why was Brazilian born soccer star Brandao, banned for six months in 2014?

2420. Who did West Indian cricketer Brian Lara surpass to become the highest scorer in an innings of a test match when he scored 400 not out in 2004?

2421. In which country is there a rugby league team known as the Scarborough Centurions ?

2422. Which horse achieved the following wins in 1880: AJC Derby, AJC Mares Produce Stakes, VRC Mares Produce Stakes, The Melbourne Cup and the VRC Victoria Derby?

2423. Who was the first black tennis player to win a singles championship title at a Grand Slam tournament?

2424. Who captained the AFL's Sydney Swans from 1993 until 2002?

2425. Who was the player who won the "Golden Ball" award and captained France in the association football World Cup of 2006?

2426. What is the name of the medal awarded to the best player afield in a Victorian Football League grand final?

2427. Where were the Pan Pacific swimming championships held in August 2014?

2428. Who won the Stawell Easter Gift in 1966 and 1967?

2429. Which English association football league club are known as "The Owls"?

2430. Australian Sam Willoughby is a champion in which sport?

2431. With which sport is Australian William Power associated?

2432. What was the name of the mascot for the 1994 Commonwealth Games in Victoria, Canada?

2433. Who won the "Laureus World Sportsman of the Year" award for four consecutive years from 2005 to 2008?

2434. Pastor Maldonado and Valtteri Bottas were the 2013 Formula One drivers for which team?

2435. Who was the inaugural coach of the Australian NBL team, the Gold Coast Blaze?

2436. The New Jersey Devils are within which division of the Eastern Conference of the North American National Hockey League?

2437. In cricket, what is a "dot ball"?

2438. Who was the Australian A-League (NSL) player who won the Johnny Warren Medal in 1993-1994 and again in 1994-1995?

2439. Who was the captain of the West Indian cricket team that tied a test match with Australia at the Gabba in December 1960?

2440. In which year did the West Indies play their first cricket test match?

2441. The national English rugby league team are also known by what nickname?

2442. Which horse that sired Kingston Town?

2443. Who was the first women's singles champion at Wimbledon?

2444. Who was the boxer who knocked out Jake Rodriguez in Las Vegas Nevada in 1995 to become the IBF light welterweight world champion?

2445. Who was the player who kicked the winning behind to win the AFL's preliminary final against Essendon in 1996?

2446. French footballer Patrick Vieira played for which two English Premier League clubs?

2447. In which state did St Kilda (AFL) player Nick Riewoldt play his junior and early senior football?

2448. How many seasons was John Worsfold captain of the AFL's West Coast Eagles?

2449. Which yacht was declared overall winner of the 2015 Sydney to Hobart yacht race?

2450. Who were the two players who won the women's Australian tennis Open doubles title in January 2015?

2451. The Buffalo Sabres are within which division of the Eastern Conference of the North American National Hockey League?

2452. Which team did Perth Heat defeat to win the 2014 baseball championship?

2453. Who was the former St Kilda (AFL) player who coached the South Australian National Football League side Central Districts between 1984 and 1987?

2454. What is the name given to the fourth hole at the Augusta National Golf course, home of the U.S. Masters?

2455. Who was the Australian National Basketball League's "Coach of the Year" in 2009, 2008, 2002, 1998 and 1992?

2456. Which team was Michael Doohan riding for when he won the MotoGP championship from 1994 to 98?

2457. What is the nickname of the Australian Hockey League men's team from Tasmania?

2458. Motor cycle champion Casey Stoner won his first world championship riding for which team?

2459. Who was coach of South Australian National Football League club Central Districts between 2001 and 2002?

2460. In which year did India play their first cricket test match?

2461. What place in the north of England is considered to be the birth place of rugby league?

2462. Who rode the racehorse Kingston Town for 25 of his 30 wins?

2463. How much should a new tennis ball weigh?

2464. With which club did Roy Cazaly make his AFL/VFL debut in 1911?

2465. Ruud van Nistelrooy is a professional footballer who has played for Real Madrid, Manchester United, Hamburger SV and Malaga among others. What is his country of origin?

2466. Which two National League Baseball teams did player Willie Mays play with during his career?

2467. Who won rugby union's John Eales Medal in 2007?

2468. What type of delivery in cricket was accredited to test cricketer Clarrie Grimmett?

2469. Which team did Australia play in 1989 in the first ever cricket test held at Hobart's Bellerive Oval?

2470. Who was the Australian National Soccer League player who won the Johnny Warren Medal twice while playing with the Wollongong Wolves?

2471. What "cricket first" did Billy Midwinter achieve in the Australian team in 1878 in a match against Nottinghamshire?

2472. Up to 2014, how many FINA World Cups have the Australian women's national water polo team won?

2473. Who was the AFL number one draft pick of 2001 and was the winner of the Norm Smith Medal in 2008 ?

2474. Where were the Winter Olympic Games held in 1972?

2475. Which team won the Australian NBL grand final in 1979?

2476. Where was former Fremantle (AFL) and North Melbourne (AFL) player Peter Bell born?

2477. Who won the men's singles final at the 2013 U.S tennis Open?

2478. Who is the only first class cricketer to have won a Nobel Prize?

2479. Which American National Ice Hockey league team is based in Sunrise, Miami Florida?

2480. In which year did New Zealand play their first cricket test match?

2481. By what name does the national rugby league side of Fiji go by?

2482. Who was the Australian race caller known as "The Accurate One"?

2483. In which year were the first women's French tennis championships held?

2484. Who was appointed coach of the Sydney Swans midway through the 2002 season?

2485. Which two European association football clubs did Dutchman Marco van Basten play for?

2486. Which English Premier League club was managed by Nigel Pearson in 2014-15?

2487. What is the division in boxing where the participants weigh is between 76.2kg and 79.4kg ?

2488. Which English championship league team are known as the Tangerines?

2489. In horse sport,what is a cavaletti?

2490. What is the nickname of the Australian futsal team?

2491. Who was the captain of the A-League side Western Sydney Wanderers during the 2014-15 season?

2492. Who was the Italian world heavyweight champion who was known as the "Ambling Alp".He held the heavyweight title from June 1933 to June 1934 after gaining it from Jack Sharkey?

2493. Who was the coach of the A-League side Brisbane Roar during the 2014-15 season?

2494. What is a Sipi Tau?

2495. What NBA team play their home games at "The Garden"?

2496. What was the name of the 100 to 1 chance winner of the 1936 Melbourne Cup?

2497. Which team was Casey Stoner representing when he won the riders MotoGP world title in 2007?

2498. Who was the AFL player who won the "Rising Star" award in 1998, and was a member of a premiership team in 1999 and 2004?

2499. Who won the men's singles final at the French tennis Open in 2013?

2500. In which year did Pakistan play their first cricket test match?

Answers

1. 1877

2. 1907

3. Peter Pan

4. Australia

5. Paoa "Duke" Kahanamoku

6. Jerry Quarry

7. Pakistan

8. Berlin, Germany

9. Footscray (Western Bulldogs)

10. 1863

11. he is credited as being the inventor of basketball (in 1891)

12. The International Olympic Committee

13. the large main group of riders in a bicycle race

14. he won the first world formula one motor racing championship

15. 1930 (Hamilton Canada)

16. Belgrade (Yugoslavia)

17. 1945

18. France (Chamonix)

19. France

20. Harry Boyle

21. May 9th 1909

22. Kyogle

23. French, Australian, U.S. and Wimbledon

24. 1983

25. 1872

26. Darren Clarke of Northern Ireland

27. Switzerland (Lucerne)

28. 7

29. 1877

30. National League (NL) and the American League (AL)

31. 1949

32. billiards

33. 32

34. The Stanley Cup

35. Rugby union (World Cup)

36. Paris, 1924

37. Grenoble, France

38. U.S Masters, British Open, U.S. Open and U.S. PGA Championship

39. she was the first woman to swim the English Channel.

40. Ivo Bligh

41. 1895

42. 6 - 1875, 1880, 1882, 1884, 1886 and 1887

43. Stade Roland Garros

44. Kelly Slater (U.S.)

45. The Football Association (FA) Cup

46. Peter Norman

47. George

48. Phillip Island in Victoria

49.   1859

50.   1878

51.   Linda McGill

52.   100 metres 200 metres, 4 x 100 metres relay and the long jump

53.   Karrie Webb

54.   Coolangatta Gold

55.   England, France, Scotland, Wales, Ireland and Italy

56.   Australian, Robert de Castella

57.   Dr W. G. Grace

58.   Dame Pattie

59.   Luge, Bobsleigh and Skeleton

60.   Bramall Lane in Sheffield, England

61.   Rugby league football

62.   2,400 metres

63.   1905

64.   11

65.   Joe Frazier

66. Birmingham, England

67. 1895 at Newport Country Club, New Port Rhode Island, U.S.A.

68. Edwin Moses

69. Carlton, Collingwood, Essendon, Fitzroy, Geelong, Melbourne St Kilda and South Melbourne

70. 200 metres, 400 metres and 800 metres freestyle

71. The Claxton Shield

72. Berlin, 1936

73. they have all won the Stawell Easter Gift

74. 1973

75. Australia, New Zealand, Argentina and South Africa

76. The Olyroos

77. Equestrian

78. Heather McKay of Australia

79. Australian, Michael Doohan

80. Victor Trumper, 103 verse England in 1902

81. 1908

82. Darren Beadman

83. 1881

84. Stephanie Gilmore (Australia)

85. a white jersey with red dots

86. Paris, 1904

87. Ayrton Senna

88. Curling

89. Essendon

90. 1936 at Garmisch-Partenkirchen in Germany

91. Horace Rawlins in 1895

92. Los Angeles 1984

93. figure skating

94. American, Dick Fosbury (Fosbury Flop)

95. Australia, New Zealand and South Africa

96. Cycling(Duncan Gray-1000m time trial), Rowing (Henry Pearce men's singles sculls) and swimming (Clare Dennis-women's 200 metre breaststroke)

97. figure skating

98. American Billy Mills

99. Soviet swimmer, Vladimir Salnikov

100. South Africa

101. Herbert "Dally" Messenger

102. Bonecrusher 2: 35: 60

103. The All England Lawn Tennis Club

104. Layne Beachley (Australia)

105. Brazil

106. Bobby Pearce

107. Australian, Shelly Taylor-Smith

108. Australia

109. 1925

110. St Louis 1904

111. Albert Trott:1895 Played 3 matches, 3 not out in 5 innings, 205 runs with a highest score of 85 not out.

112. 1,500 metres

113. Bloomington, Illinois U.S.A.

114. John J. McDerrmott in 1911

115. 1906

116. Mexico City 1968

117. Carlton, Melbourne and North Melbourne

118. Berlin 1936

119. he became the youngest player to play AFL/VFL at 15 years and 287 days

120. Warwick Armstrong

121. Alex Burdon

122. 1957

123. Australian and U.S. Opens

124. 1979, 1980, 1981 and 1982

125. Russia

126. Warren Ralph playing for Carlton verses North Melbourne

127. he became the first Australian to play Major League Baseball playing with the St Louis Maroons

128.   Pittsburgh Steelers

129.   1906

130.   Everton

131.   Joe Frazier

132.   Tony Modra verses Richmond 1993 and verses Carlton 1994

133.   Equestrian

134.   Patrick Johnson 9.93 in Japan in 2003

135.   1998

136.   Michael Fitzpatrick – Western Australian footballer (Subiaco) and Carlton captain

137.   Geoff Ogilvy

138.   Englishman, Steve Ovett

139.   Ray Gabelich

140.   South Melbourne

141.   1910

142.   Poseidon

143.   U.S. Open

144. South Africa

145. England and Scotland in 1872

146. Australian Susie Maroney

147. she won gold in the 200m breaststroke at the age of 14 and 6 days becoming the youngest gold medallist in swimming at an Olympics.

148. Jim Hines (U.S.) 1968 Olympics

149. 1902

150. 5,000m and 10,000m

151. Salzburg in Austria

152. Sapporo, Hokkaido Japan

153. Colin Ridgeway

154. Ben Graham NFL (New York Jets leadership group)

155. The Calcutta Cup

156. Lance "Buddy" Franklin (Hawthorn 2008)

157. American baseballer, Babe Ruth

158. he was the first Australian to appear in a FA Cup final when he played for Preston North End against West Bromwich Albion

159. The Players Championship, played at the Sawgrass Country Club Florida since 1982

160. Archie Jackson

161. Glebe, 9th January 1908. Newton was formed on the 14th of January 1908

162. 2006, 2007

163. The French Open

164. Peru

165. Great Britain

166. Neil Robinson

167. Equestrian

168. an Albatross

169. Leon Spinks

170. 1900

171. 20

172. England, at Sydney 3rd test

173. the Los Angeles Dodgers

174. 6

175. 139

176. they are among the group of athletes that have carried the Australian flag at Summer Olympic Games opening ceremonies

177. he was the first man to clear 7 feet in the high jump

178. 244

179. Gary Player

180. 18 and 1

181. Newtown

182. Ming Dynasty

183. 1969

184. Lisa Andersen (U.S.)

185. Uruguay had won the Olympic tournaments in 1924 and 1928 and were therefore considered to be the world champions. It was also to celebrate their centenary of independence

186. she became the first woman to light the Olympic cauldron. (Mexico City Olympics)

187. 11

188. Fulham

189. Reginald "Tip" Foster

190. 1909

191. they have all won gold medals at the Olympic Games in diving. Mitcham (2008). Newbery (2004) and Eve (1924)

192. Babe (Didrikson) Zaharius

193. Bobby Despotovski

194. 2002

195. 97

196. motor racing

197. Melbourne

198. 1959

199. Middlesbrough

200. only once

201. 9

202. AJC Australian Oaks

203. 1925

204.   Tom Carroll of Australia

205.   13, four from Europe, seven from South America and two
        from North America

206.   Andrew Murray "Boy" Charlton

207.   David Graham in 1981

208.   Briton, Steve Cram

209.   Iain Murray

210.   1920

211.   Ralph Doubell

212.   Berlin 1936

213.   snowboarding

214.   4 times - 1992, 1995, 1996, 1998

215.   Matthew Burke

216.   women's triathlon

217.   Leon Spinks

218.   super-bike racing

219.   South African, Barry Richards

220.   340 not out verses Victoria at the SCG

221.   South Sydney, 1908 and 1909

222.   AJC Queen Elisabeth Stakes

223.   1968

224.   Quicksilver

225.   1961

226.   Argentina

227.   Ian Redpath and Greg Chappell of Australia and Brian
        Luckhurst and John Edrich of England

228.   St John's Wood

229.   Muhammad Ali

230.   Jack Nicklaus

231.   the Sydney Cricket Ground

232.   John Konrads

233.   Linford Christie of Great Britain

234.   Bert Thornely

235.   Michael Lynagh

236.   The Jilleroos

237.   water polo

238.   Stephen Kernahan, Carlton

239.   Carlton player Bruce Doull

240.   3rd test in Melbourne 1928-29 (112)

241.   1915

242.   Morphetville, Adelaide in April

243.   Flushing Meadow-Corona Park in Queens, New York

244.   Bernard "Midget" Farrelly

245.   Uruguay

246.   1966

247.   12

248.   American, Mary Lou Retton (Los Angeles 1984)

249.   The Championship (The Football League Championship)

250.   90 times

251.   long jump, 100 metres, 200 metres and 4 X 100 metre relay

252. he was the oldest person to play VFL/AFL football at the age of 43 years

253. Alan Shearer

254. Willie Anderson

255. 25

256. Dale Kickett

257. Cliff Lyons (1987), Geoff Toovey (1996) and Brent Kite (2008) Glenn Stewart (2011) and Daly Cherry-Evans (2013)

258. Cardiff City's Robert Earnshaw

259. Ken Norton

260. 131

261. 1921

262. Northerly

263. strawberries and cream

264. 4 times

265. 1991 in People's Republic of China

266. 1975

267.   Stephen Fleming (Australia)

268.   9 (1956, 1958, 1960, 1961, 1962, 1963, 1964, 1968 and 1969)

269.   Darren Lehmann

270.   Michael Wenden

271.   Terry Lamb

272.   Glen Boss

273.   Mickey Mantle

274.   a Kenyan athlete who was the winner of the Beijing Olympic
        marathon. He died in a fall from his apartment balcony in
        2011 at the age of 24 following a domestic dispute.

275.   64

276.   Graeme Wood and Rick Darling

277.   Ernie Els and Retief Goosen

278.   Australian Dean Lukin

279.   Wayne Grady and Peter Fowler

280.   1930-31

281.   1930

282. Vo Rogue

283. 1868

284. Ian Cairns and Peter Townsend

285. he was the designer of the World Cup trophy

286. 1992

287. Boston Celtic

288. the Leigh Matthews trophy

289. Andrew Bogut

290. Innsbruck, Austria

291. 24

292. Stephen Hendry

293. Melbourne F.C.

294. Kolkata Knight Riders

295. Daisuke Ohata of Japan with 69

296. 21, 20 for Western Australia and 1 for Victoria

297. David Nilsson and Grant Balfour

298. Stefan Edberg and Hanna Mandlikova

299. 13

300. Bill Bowes

301. Eastern Suburbs

302. Flemington in Melbourne

303. a pioneer of the game of lawn tennis

304. three times, 1985,1986 and 1990

305. 4: 1934, 1938, 1982 and 2006

306. 1997

307. Jon Sieben

308. Sydney Thunder

309. 6

310. Eritrea

311. Joe DiMaggio

312. Roy Higgins

313. New South Wales and Western Australia

314.   Golden Point

315.   Australian David Campese

316.   Brian Smith

317.   Eric Cantona for Leeds against Tottenham Hotspur, August
        1992

318.   Matilda

319.   Augusta National Golf Club in Augusta Georgia U.S.A.

320.   Bill Ponsford

321.   1938

322.   Northerly

323.   Fred Perry of England

324.   "White Lightning"

325.   5: 1958, 1962, 1970, 1994, 2002

326.   Brisbane Lions

327.   a score of 111 or its multiples

328.   Lyn McClements

329.   Wenlock and Manderville,

330.   golf; these are all old names for various clubs ie. Brassie- 2 wood, a niblick- 9 iron, jigger- low lofting iron, a mashie- 5 iron and a cleek -2 iron

331.   Englishmen, Graham and Damon Hill

332.   Derek Chadwick

333.   Portsmouth and Coventry City

334.   1981

335.   New Zealand and Australia

336.   track walking

337.   Bob Pratt (South Melbourne 1934) and Peter Hudson (Hawthorn 1971)

338.   1976 (Ornskoldsvik in Sweden)

339.   Louise Sauvage

340.   Gubby Allen

341.   Western Suburbs

342.   1,200 metres for two year olds

343.   1900

344.   Mark Occhilupo (Australia)

345. George Foreman

346. 2004

347. 4, 1954, 1974, 1990, 2014

348. Gary Player of South Africa in 1961

349. Boston, Berlin, New York, London and Chicago

350. Kyra Yuill riding Western Jewel

351. Liam Davis

352. Maureen Caird

353. they played test cricket for both Australia and England

354. he was the first male to complete the Western Australian mainland to Rottnest Island swim

355. South Africa

356. Volleyball

357. 1986

358. Houston Texans

359. Steve Moneghetti

360. Stan McCabe

361. 4

362. Scobie Breasley

363. 28

364. Easter time

365. 2, 1978 and 1986

366. 1871

367. Peru. Tactu Golf Club in Morococha

368. pole vaulting

369. she became the first woman to reach the top of Mount Everest

370. Korean: Sohn Kee Chung (gold) and Nam Sung-yong (silver) ran for Japan under Japanese names

371. Pele , (the former Brazilian soccer star)

372. Jack Nicklaus with 6: 1963, 1965, 1966, 1972, 1975 and 1986

373. Glynis Nunn, Australia

374. archery

375. "Swing Low Sweet Chariot"

376. Korea

377.   Mozambique

378.   Hungry in 1953   6-3

379.   baseball

380.   1947-48

381.   University

382.   Bart Cummings

383.   Milton Courts, Brisbane

384.   Reef Hawaiian Pro, O'Neill World Cup of Surfing and the Billabong Pipeline Masters

385.   Germany (4-2)

386.   1883

387.   South Melbourne

388.   No. 3

389.   Everton F.C.

390.   Boxing

391.   11

392.   a Turkey

393. he became the first black Major League player of the modern era.

394. NHL (ice hockey)

395. the red rose

396. October 1860

397. Pato; a game played on horse back which combines the elements of polo and basketball

398. South African Hansie Cronje

399. in a pool or in water (volleyball in water)

400. 99.94

401. Western Suburbs

402. 6 years old

403. 1988

404. Kieren Perrow

405. Sweden

406. 1892

407. Berlin, Germany

408. Rani

409. England

410. F.C. Porto (Portugal)

411. Indianapolis Colts

412. Larry Holmes

413. Real Madrid

414. UEFA Super Cup

415. rugby union and cricket

416. Shaquille O'Neal

417. Americans Charles and Chip Jenkins for the 400 metres relay (Charles at the 1956 Melbourne Olympics and Chip at the 1992 Barcelona Olympics)

418. Boston Celtic

419. Frenchman Arnaud Massy

420. he dismissed Don Bradman for a duck in Bradman's last innings denying him a test average of 100

421. Parramatta and St George (St George won the replay)

422. Rogilla

423. Rod Laver

424. Eastern Cape in South Africa

425. 3, 1974, 1978 and 2010

426. 1864

427. Syd (1890) and Ned Gregory (1877)

428. the Adelaide Oval

429. Middlebrough

430. Lake Placid New York USA

431. South Sydney

432. she became the first woman to run across Australia's Simpson Desert, completing the 660km journey in 10 days.

433. a World Cup qualifying match in 1996 against Moldova

434. Sri Lankan, Lasith Malinga (2007 against South Africa)

435. rugby union and cricket

436. Besart Berisha

437. Sebastian Vettel

438. Trent Durrington

439. Hawthorn

440. Lindsay Hassett

441. 1989, defeating Balmain

442. Might and Power

443. 11

444. Kelly Slater (U.S.)

445. Pele: Brazil, 1958, 1962 and 1970

446. 1874

447. Peter Thomson

448. the men's 4000m team pursuit in cycling

449. after her death in 1980, an autopsy revealed that she had male genitalia

450. 25

451. Keith Barnes

452. men's triple jump

453. Paralympic gold medallist 1500m and 400m wheelchair

454. Deborah Bowman

455.   Leicester Tigers

456.   Targa West 06

457.   Thierry Henry

458.   Wayne Carey

459.   Kit the Cat

460.   Arsenal

461.   Balmain, their opponent, refused to take the field as a protest against having the match placed as a warm up match for a Kangaroos /Wallaby game.

462.   Super Impose

463.   Richard "Pancho" Gonzales

464.   Peru

465.   25

466.   1885

467.   Noel Cleal

468.   Chris "Choppy" Close

469.   1986 and 1993

470. 20

471. American, Florence Griffith-Joyner

472. 9

473. Blue Bird (CN7)

474. Trap (shooting)

475. Saracens

476. Rome, 1960

477. Tripoli, Lebanon

478. 9

479. Englishman John Edrich in the sixth test in Adelaide of the 1970-71 series

480. Peter May

481. 11

482. Gunsynd

483. Romania

484. Wayne Bartholomew

485. 15

486.   1859

487.   San Antonio Spurs

488.   field hockey (1956 Olympic team)

489.   45 years

490.   Lou Gehrig

491.   Mark Kerry, Neil Brooks, Mark Tonelli and Peter Evans

492.   16

493.   PGA Championship

494.   Nova Peris-Kneebone, field hockey player at Atlanta in 1996

495.   The Brumbies

496.   Kevin Gosper

497.   Trevor Gillmeister

498.   an Eagle

499.   Salford City Reds

500.   22

501.   Cumberland

502. 1,350 metres

503. 8

504. Australian, Simon Anderson

505. 13

506. 1883

507. South Africa (Johannesburg)

508. Equestrian (Mixed dressage championship Grade III and mixed dressage freestyle grade III)

509. Newtown and North Sydney

510. Marathon

511. Germany (89 medals , 33 gold, 26 silver, and 30 bronze)

512. former Brisbane Roar coach Ange Postecoglou

513. St Kilda player Nicky Winmar

514. Israel

515. The Waratahs

516. Crews for the Oxford -Cambridge boat race

517. David Graham (1979), Wayne Grady (1990) and Steve

Elkington (1995)

518. Canadian, Ben Johnson

519. Liverpool

520. India

521. Eastern Suburbs(Sydney Roosters) and South Sydney (Rabbitohs)

522. Might and Power

523. 12

524. Lynne Boyer (U.S.)

525. Geoff Hurst

526. 1902

527. Jose Mourinho

528. Stephen Milne

529. Jacksonville, Florida

530. Japan

531. Alexander Dale Oen

532. long jump

533. 2

534. Phil Jackson

535. Queensland Reds

536. John Aloisi

537. Blackburn Rovers

538. Fred Kersley

539. Jim Ferrier in 1947 (PGA match play)

540. William Gilbert

541. Glebe

542. Chatham

543. Fred Stolle

544. Mark Foo

545. they have both played in and been head coach of a winning World Cup side.

546. 1873

547. Australian rules and baseball

548. Lionel Messi

549. 1993

550. the Goodwood at Morphettville in South Australia

551. Barcelona 1992

552. Manuka Oval in Canberra

553. Pink

554. Port Adelaide

555. Brumbies

556. Jamaica (Usain Bolt, Yohan Blake, Michael Frater and Nesta Carter 37.04)

557. 3 times, 1994-95, 1995-96, 1996-97

558. Queens Park Rangers

559. 4, 1999, 2000, 2006 and 2007

560. Joe Darling

561. Western Suburbs Magpies

562. 1,600 metres

563. Arthur Ashe

564. George Freeth

565. he coached Italy to two World Cup wins, 1934 and 1938

566. 1869

567. he became the first Venezuelan to win a Formula One motor Grand Prix by winning the Spanish Grand Prix.

568. 2-0 in favour of Australia

569. 9

570. the taekwondo competitor deliberately kicked a referee in the face and punched an official

571. Sid "Joe" Pearce (1932) and Sandy Pearce (1908)

572. Chilean

573. Melbourne's Ron Barassi Senior, killed at Tobruk in North Africa

574. London 1948

575. Western Force

576. Italian, Marco Simoncelli

577. boxer Mike Tyson

578. U.S.A

579. 800m 1:41:01

580. Sachin Tendulkar

581. Annandale

582. Golden Slipper Stakes

583. Ivan Lendl

584. 6

585. the Golden Boot award for being top goal scorer with 13 goals for the finals tournament

586. 1987

587. Jim Barnes (England)

588. Chris Munce

589. Orlando Magic

590. Fishing

591. 1829 (won by Oxford)

592. Holden VE Commodore

593. American boxer Mike Tyson

594. Rory McIlroy

595. Melbourne Rebels (rugby union)

596. American golfer Tiger Woods

597. Bayern Munich

598. high jump (2.45m)

599. Essendon's forward Leroy Jetta

600. 52

601. Manly-Warringah Sea Eagles forming the Northern Sea Eagles

602. Shane Dye

603. 7

604. she became the first woman world surfing champion

605. Germany's Thomas Muller

606. 1991

607. Sydney Showground Stadium

608. Australian Mark Webber

609. Gerry Cooney

610. 7, (1958, 1962, 1963, 1965, 1969, 1970, 1974)

611. Fremantle Dockers

612.   he became the first Canadian to win a cycling "Grand Tour" event by winning the Giro d'Italia.

613.   Lewis Hamilton

614.   Sara Errani

615.   The Blues

616.   Port Adelaide

617.   Webb Simpson

618.   bad sportsmanship after he kicked an advertising sign onto the leg of an official.

619.   Russia

620   334 not out

621.   Annandale

622.   LKS MacKinnon Stakes

623.   8

624.   Huntington Beach California

625.   Sheffield Football Club in England

626.   1987

627. Jorge Lorenzo

628. Match Play

629. Andy Zhang

630. Fanny Blankers-Koen

631. Tino Best

632. Lukas Rosol

633. Mario Balotelli

634. Graeme Lloyd with the Atlanta Braves

635. The Chiefs of New Zealand

636. Casey Stoner

637. Denver Broncos

638. 4-0

639. she became the first Pole since 1937 to reach a Wimbledon ladies singles final.

640. 1,107

641. 1967

642. Moonee Valley, (Melbourne in September)

643. 18

644. Nico Rosberg

645. Birmingham

646. 1996

647. Queensland's Nate Myles

648. Serena Williams

649. Headingly and Edgbaston

650. Jamaican/Canadian Trevor Berbick in 1981

651. 400m 43.18

652. Serbian tennis player Novak Djokovic

653. 9

654. Darren Clarke UK/Northern Ireland

655. 7

656. Bunny Austin, 1938 (runner up)

657. Greater Western Sydney

658. Andy Murray

659.   Australian, Mark Webber

660.   27

661.   1947

662.   the Manikato Stakes

663.   22

664.   Goofy

665.   Aston Villa

666.   1982

667.   Glasgow Rangers

668.   Bradley Wiggins

669.   Fernando Alonso

670.   17

671.   Hashim Amla 311 not out (July 22nd 2012 verses England at the Oval in London)

672.   James Magnussen

673.   Basketballer Lauren Jackson

674.   Kenya

675. Dunedin, New Zealand

676. 22   (eighteen gold , two silver and two bronze)

677. fencing

678. Rory McIlroy

679. Anchorage and Nome in Alaska

680. Darren Lehmann, South Australia/Victoria

681. 1988

682. John Cutts

683. 18

684. China

685. Liverpool

686. 1870

687. horse racing- she is a record breaking female jockey

688. Zero

689. Collingwood

690. Oxford and Cambridge university boat race

691. Kansas City Chiefs

692. Oxford and Cambridge universities

693. Czechoslovakia in 1980

694. he was the winner of the first New York marathon

695. Wellington, New Zealand

696. Alessandro Del Piero

697. Serena Williams

698. triple jump (18.29 metres)

699. Discus

700. 110.19

701. 1988

702. Black Caviar

703. 18

704. 16

705. Barcelona

706. 1997

707. Lewis Hamilton

708. 5,(1980, 1985, 1987, 1995, 1996)

709. American John Tate

710. 5th

711. St Kilda's Nicky Winmar

712. Carlton's Wayne Johnston

713. Danny Nicolik

714. Fiveandahalfstar

715. The Bulls

716. International Boxing Organisation cruiserweight title against New Zealander Shane Cameron

717. Sebastian Vettel

718. Gallic Roaster

719. Mr Moet

720. 355 not out

721. Gold Coast-Tweedheads Giants

722. 1,200 metres

723. they have all won Grand Slam singles titles on grass, clay and hardcourts

724. Michael Peterson

725. Celtic

726. 1995

727. Scotland and Ireland

728. 28

729. Tom-Jelte Slagter

730. San Francisco 49's and the Baltimore Ravens

731. she was the first coloured woman and African American woman to win an Olympic gold medal.

732. The Grand National at Aintree

733. Australian, Adam Scott

734. 6, (1964, 1968, 1971, 1975, 1976, 1978)

735. The Cheetahs

736. Goldfinger

737. Royal Randwick, Sydney

738.   Faf du Plessis

739.   Barakey

740.   159 (Western Australia and South Australia)

741.   Gold Coast-Tweedheads Giants, Gold Coast Seagulls and Gold Coast Chargers

742.   Caulfield

743.   17

744.   Sally Fitzgibbons

745.   Real Madrid

746.   2011

747.   Glen Boss

748.   Oakland Raiders, San Diego Chargers and the San Francisco 49ers

749.   Brisbane Heat

750.   American basketballer Michael Jordan.

751.   Ashleigh Barty

752.   Marta

753. Madagascar runner , Jean-Louis Ravelomanantsoa

754. Brazilian Grand Prix

755. The Stormers

756. Royal Descent

757. Central Coast

758. Josh Kennedy

759. French woman Marion Bartoli and German Sabine Lisicki

760. 452 not out verses Queensland

761. Canberra and Illawarra

762. Queen of the Turf Stakes

763. Rafael Nadal

764. Van's Hawaiian Pro, the Roxy Pro and the Billabong Pro Maui

765. 19 years

766. Nottingham Forest

767. Green Moon

768. Brisbane Lions

769.	Overreach

770.	Andy Murray of Britain

771.	Valerie Adams of New Zealand for the women's shot put

772.	Mark Cavendish

773.	Phil Mickleson

774.	Sebastian Vettel

775.	The Lions

776.	American Mike Weaver

777.	Victoria Azarenka

778.	British rider Victoria Pendleton

779.	Gold Coast's Gary Ablett

780.	Clarrie Grimmett (South Australia and Victoria)

781.	1980

782.	Gayndah

783.	Novak Djokovic

784.	Hossegor, France

785. Fitzroy

786. Leeds United

787. Coupe Suzanne Lenglen

788. Jimmy Spithill

789. Manly's Daly Cherry-Evans

790. St Kilda's Darrell Baldock

791. Ukrainian, Vladimir Klitschko

792. Spaniard, Marc Marquez

793. Adam Scott

794. West Indies

795. The Sharks

796. Adam Scott

797. Perth Scorchers

798. La Perouse

799. Korean

800. 338

801. North Brisbane, South Brisbane, Toombul and Valley

802. Queensland Oaks (possible name change to Doomben Roses)

803. 17

804. Mick Fanning of Australia

805. Australian Rules Football

806. Manchester United

807. Melbourne Storm's Cooper Cronk

808. Lleyton Hewitt

809. Michael Dokes

810. Gary Marocchi

811. Spain, Chile and the Netherlands

812. Karak, the red tailed black cockatoo

813. West Perth

814. Jonah Lomu

815. The Brumbies

816. Ian Baker-Finch

817. Western Australia and Tasmania

818. Geelong (1995-1999) and Adelaide (2000-2004)

819. rugby league (Brisbane Broncos, Canberra Raiders and Australia)

820. A.A. Mailey 4/362 for NSW verses Victoria in 1926

821. 1922

822. Northerly

823. Pete Sampras

824. Pam Burridge

825. Collingwood

826. Arsenal (2006) and Chelsea (2008)

827. Madrid and Istanbul

828. Argentina

829. No. 6

830. one year

831. John Winter- men's high jump and Mervyn Wood – men's single sculls in rowing

832.   Travis Dodd

833.   Dunaden

834.   Australia's Michael Clarke

835.   Waratahs

836.   Steve Smith 138 no

837.   Australian, Mick Fanning

838.   Eton and Harrow (began 1805)

839.   two (West Indian Ivan Burrow 1930 and
        Wally Hammond 1933)

840.   10 for 36 by T.W. Wall for South Australia verses NSW
        in 1933

841.   the Brisbane Exhibition Ground

842.   Morphetville, South Australia

843.   Lleyton Hewitt

844.   boxing

845.   Carlton

846.   Juventus

847. Nagambie

848. Ken Arthurson

849. New Zealand's Sonny Bill Williams

850. The Dallas Cowboys

851. Wild Oats XI

852. Adam Scott

853. Graham Arthur

854. Caroline Buchanan

855. Queensland Reds

856. Unencumbered

857. J-league second division side Consadole Sapporo

858. 6th

859. Jamie Whincup and Paul Dumbrell

860. Ian Brayshaw for Western Australia verses Victoria

861. Fortitude Valley Diehards

862. 3,200 metres

863. they have all been coached by Australian Tony Roche

864. Boxing

865. South Melbourne (Sydney Swans)

866. Arsenal

867. London 2012

868. Sailing

869. Old Trafford

870. 100 metres hurdles and the 80 metres hurdles

871. Association footballer Cristiano Ronaldo

872. Daniel Ricciardo

873. Mitchell Johnson

874. Eric Cantona

875. The Cheetahs (16-14)

876. Seattle Seahawks

877 the Mackinnon Stakes

878. Jacob Willcox

879. Stuart Broad

880. D.S. Berry (South Australia and Victoria)

881. Redcliffe Dolphins

882. Tie the Knot

883. 3:1967, 1970, 1971

884. Marquess of Queensbury Rules

885. Richmond Tigers

886. Blackburn Rovers

887. Clayton Zane

888. France

889. because of the once bony appearance of the sled.

890. Dermott Brereton

891. Lankan Rupee

892. Dani Pedrosa

893. Chumpy

894. Japan's J-league

895.   Edward "Weary" Dunlop (1932)

896.   Canada and Sweden

897.   WBA/ IBF/IBO/WBO heavyweight boxing champion of the world

898.   Fiorente

899.   Spain

900.   Don Tallon :Queensland verses New South Wales

901.   South Africa

902.   1980

903.   1997 and 1998

904.   The London Prize Ring Rules

905.   Geelong

906.   Bolton Wanderers

907.   National and American Leagues

908.   Serena Williams

909.   Karrie Webb

910.   Shannon Eckstein

911. Jaeger O'Meara of the Gold Coast Suns

912. Bendigo Spirit

913. Shera, a royal Bengal tiger

914. Murwillumbah, New South Wales

915. Waratahs

916. Oracle Team

917. Essex (1996-2001), Lancashire (2002-2008) and Derbyshire (2009)

918. Swimmer Michael Phelps

919. Swiss, Stanislas Wawrinka

920. Jamie Siddons and John Inverarity

921. France

922. Galilee

923. 2001

924. John L. Sullivan

925. 9

926. Chelsea

927. Nico Rosberg

928. Sarajevo, Yugoslavia

929. Melbourne Storm's Cooper Cronk

930. women's vision impaired giant slalom

931. Helsinki 1952

932. Brisbane Roar

933. highest goal scorer in a grand final

934. Daniel Riccardo

935. Crusaders

936. Australian, Karrie Webb

937. Shamus Award

938. U.S. Air Force

939. New York Giants

940. 431 by M .Veletta and G. Marsh for Western Australia against South Australia in 1989

941. 41

942. Victoria Derby

943.   Andre Agassi

944.   Irish-American, Jim Corbett who defeated John L. Sullivan

945.   Hawthorn, Footscray and North Melbourne

946.   Everton

947.   Judo

948.   800 metres

949.   Australia

950.   WACA ground Perth, Western Australia

951.   Bayern Munich (association football)

952.   New Zealand

953.   Carissa Moore

954.   Daniel Geale

955.   Richie McCaw

956.   Pineau De Re

957.   Carbine

958.   Essendon's Jobe Watson

959. cricket match

960. Steve and Mark Waugh

961. 24

962. Moonee Valley in Melbourne

963. Tony Roche

964. Jack Dempsey

965. Colin Watson in 1925

966. Fulham

967. Malvolio

968. 1892

969. Les Brennen

970. he became the first aboriginal man to play in the NSW first grade rugby league premiership competition

971. Buffalo Bills

972. Bubba Watson

973. boxing (known as Broughton's rules)

974. they were all the first women in Australia to receive Life

Savings bronze medallions

975. South Africa and New Zealand

976. Surfing (Duke Kahanamoku invited her to join him on his board while he gave a surfing display at Freshwater Beach in Sydney)

977. Doug Walters

978. 37 years old

979. Sydney station 2SB

980. 307, A.F Kippax and J.E.H. Hooker, New South Wales verses Victoria 1928

981. 23

982. Takeover Target

983. Don Budge in 1938

984. Jack Dempsey

985. North Melbourne

986. Liverpool

987. 12 years old, 115 no for Bowral School against Mittagong School

988. American golfer Tiger Woods

989. Essendon, even though Richmond had beaten them in the final.

990. Sebastian Vettel

991. Adelaide United

992. 24 times

993. 2000 Sydney Olympics

994. Marjorie Jackson- 100 metres and 200 metres, Shirley Strickland- 80 metre hurdles

995. Tom Howard

996. The Winterbottom Stakes

997. Chris Froome

998. Lindsay Gaze

999. "Super Boot"

1000. 80 by Les Favell, South Australia

1001. 4

1002 The VRC Oaks

1003. Rod Laver of Australia

1004. Technical Knock Out

1005. Ron Alexander

1006. Manchester City

1007. Cliff Rankin

1008. Mick Fanning

1009. Polanski

1010. Australian, Daniel Ricciardo

1011. The Netherlands

1012. Miami Dolphins

1013. Melbourne Grammar and Scotch College

1014. at 22 years and 223 days, he became the youngest Wallaby captain since 1961.

1015. 1995

1016. T.W. Sherrin

1017. Claremont

1018. Mile Jedinak

1019. North Melbourne

1020.   Michael Bevan 32 (1990-2004)

1021.   201

1022.   10 stone 11lbs (68kgs)

1023.   Roger Federer

1024.   American, Joe Louis

1025.   9th

1026.   Manchester United

1027.   Serena Williams

1028.   Zac Purton

1029.   19 games

1030.   Australian Moto3 Grand Prix

1031.   Ugandan Stephen Kiprotich

1032.   Central Districts

1033.   leg break

1034.   1903

1035.   Joel Stransky

1036. Adelaide

1037. World Series

1038. Wayne Carey

1039. The Australian Golf Open

1040. 17

1041. 33

1042. Flight

1043. Jack Crawford

1044. Sugar Ray Robinson

1045. Graham Cornes

1046. Newcastle United and Sunderland

1047. two wickets taken off two consecutive deliveries

1048. Canberra

1049. Fitzroy

1050. Nottinghamshire County Cricket Club

1051. Hazem El Masri

1052.	Ben Dunk

1053.	Gavin Wanganeen

1054.	The Western Reds

1055.	Francois Pienaar

1056.	21

1057.	South African

1058.	Maria Sharapova

1059.	Fiorente

1060.	Greg Matthews

1061.	39

1062.	Oakey

1063.	Helen Willis Moody of the U.S.

1064.	Lennox Lewis

1065.	Peter Knights

1066.	Norwich City

1067.	The Barclays in New Jersey New York

1068. Adelaide City Eagles

1069. Charlotte Edwards

1070. Martin Johnson

1071. Brisbane Bears

1072. Mo Farah

1073. Roger Federer

1074. Adelaide 36s

1075. The Currie Cup

1076. Victorian Football Association

1077. Keith Slater

1078. New England Patriots

1079. Bruce Monteath

1080. 112.97

1081. 20

1082. Hyde Park Sydney in October 1810

1083. Maureen Connolly Brinker of the U.S. in 1953

1084. George Foreman

1085. John Northey

1086. Queens Park Rangers

1087. 1904

1088. David Morris of Australia

1089. she became the first woman to compete in the Sydney to Hobart yacht race.

1090. South Australia (Adelaide Plains Football League)

1091. Tony Mann

1092. January 1838 (at the Inn owned by John Pascoe Fawkner)

1093. Backwood

1094. Peter Sumich (West Coast Eagles)

1095. he was the founder and first president of the Barbarians Football Club

1096. Thorbjorn Olesen

1097. a shared award with Luis Suarez and Cristiano Ronaldo

1098. Oaks Day

1099. boxer, Floyd Mayweather

1100. 22

1101. 31

1102. Randwick

1103. Margaret Court of Australia

1104. Charles "Sonny" Liston

1105. 36

1106. Stoke City

1107. Abu Dhabi

1108. Hazem El Masri

1109. Brian O'Driscoll

1110. Los Angeles Galaxy

1111. a delivery where a left handed bowler bowls wrist spin

1112. Melbourne 1997-2002, Collingwood 2003-2005

1113 2005

1114. Rafael Nadal

1115.   The Barbarians

1116.   Daniel Metropolis

1117.   the Skeleton

1118.   Mike Brearley

1119.   The Lakes Golf Club, Eastlakes New South Wales

1120.   J. Cox : 30 between 1987-2005

1121.   36

1122.   1943

1123.   1960

1124.   American, Rocky Marciano

1125.   Guy McKenna

1126.   Sunderland

1127.   rugby union: the black dot is the mark at the centre of the cross
        bar connecting the goal posts. It is often used as an aiming
        spot to aid kickers

1128.   American basketballer Michael Jordan

1129.   3

1130.　Aussie rules coach John Kennedy

1131.　Jo-Wilfried Tsonga of France at the Australian Open.

1132.　Mike Osbourne

1133.　North Melbourne

1134.　18

1135.　1890, verses Hartlepool Rovers,

1136.　2,400 metres

1137.　Hazem El Masri

1138.　New York Jets

1139.　Allan Jeans

1140.　31

1141.　2010

1142.　1864

1143.　3, Australian, Wimbledon and the U.S.

1144.　Cassius Clay

1145.　Collingwood 1911 and South Melbourne 1912

1146. Swansea City

1147. David Cloke

1148. Lydia Lassila

1149. the trophy awarded to the winner of the French men's singles tennis Open

1150. Anthony Minichiello (New South Wales)

1151. Fremantle's Matt Fyth

1152. 2007

1153. 8

1154. Kevin Sheedy

1155. Australia and South Africa

1156. black and white hoops with socks the colour of the individual players home club

1157. Netball (Queensland Fire Birds)

1158. Joyce Brown

1159. 20 years old

1160. Justin Langer, 29

1161.　1989, between Widnes Vikings and the Canberra Raiders

1162.　1856

1163.　Margaret (Smith) Court

1164.　Gene Tunney

1165.　1924

1166.　Tottenham Hotspur and Arsenal

1167.　Sister Olive

1168.　John Platten (Hawthorn)

1169.　Geelong's Neville Bruns

1170.　Barnsley

1171.　Rory McIlroy

1172.　Mark Zanotti (Subiaco)

1173.　he rode in a car for 11 miles during the 26 mile marathon event

1174.　1922

1175.　1984

1176.　Claremont's Kane Mitchell

1177. 12

1178. February 1921

1179. Adelaide Oval

1180. 7

1181. 1992 and 1997 respectively

1182. 1852

1183. Steffi Graf of Germany

1184. Larry Holmes

1185. 1898

1186. West Bromwich Albion

1187. Sunline

1188. Highveld Lions

1189. women's rowing pairs

1190. New Zealand

1191. Baltimore Ravens

1192. 2002

1193.   Windbag

1194.   Nathan Hindmarsh

1195.   Bob Dwyer

1196.   Tim Watson

1197.   Bob Spargo

1198.   Luckygray

1199.   David Neitz

1200.   Jock Irvine and Ross Edwards (W.A.), 244 set in 1968 against
         New South Wales

1201.   Wigan

1202.   1863

1203.   Arantxa Sanchez Vicario

1204.   Sugar Ray Leonard

1205.   1921

1206.   Wigan Athletic

1207.   Ian Brewer

1208.   Mel Schumacher

1209   David Beckham

1210.   Cincinnati Bengals

1211.   Diego Maradona

1212.   1964

1213.   Cortina d'Ampezzo Italy

1214.   Brett Rumford

1215.   55

1216.   6 times (1987, 1988, 1990, 1991, 1992 and 1994)

1217.   Marty Clarke

1218.   Terry Alderman

1219.   Trevor Allan

1220.   he took 7 catches for the match

1221.   Kevin Walters and Michael Hancock

1222.   1874

1223.   Steffi Graf

1224.   Muhammad Ali and Joe Frasier

1225. Hayden Bunton Senior; (Fitzroy, 1931, 1932,and 1935), Dick Reynolds, Essendon, (1934, 1937, and 1938); Bob Skelton, (South Melbourne, 1959, 1963 and 1968); Ian Stewart St Kilda and Richmond,(1965, 1966 and 1971)

1226. Wolverhampton Wanderers

1227. John Longmire

1228. 14

1229. Fiji in Canberra in 2010

1230. Italian, Valentino Rossi

1231. 15

1232. Ron Evans

1233. Madi Robinson of the Melbourne Vixens

1234. Western Australian Greg Chalmers

1235. they have all been members of a team that has won the World Cup twice.

1236. Kelly Slater

1237. Named after an Indian cricketer named Vinoo Mankad who ran out a player at the bowler's end as he was about to deliver a ball, first done in the second test against Australia in Sydney in 1947.

1238.   Cristiano Ronaldo

1239.   George Bernard Shaw

1240.   Graeme Wood and John Inverarity

1241.   Allan Langer, Brisbane Broncos

1242.   Scobie Breasley

1243.   Monica Seles

1244.   Mike Tyson, 20 years, 4 months and 22 days

1245.   9:Peter Moore (Collingwood -Melbourne 79, 84);
        Chris Judd (West Coast and Carlton 2004,2010);Adam Goodes
        (Sydney 2003, 2006); Robert Harvey (St Kilda 97, 98); Greg
        Williams (Sydney and Carlton 86, 94); Keith Grieg(North
        Melbourne 73, 74); Roy Wright (Richmond 52, 54); Bill
        Hutchison (Essendon 52, 53) and Ivor Warne-Smith
        (Melbourne 26, 28)

1246.   1871-1872 season

1247.   Fawkner

1248.   Arsenal

1249.   North Melbourne

1250.   England's Steve Davis

1251.   Mick Cronin

1252. 1984

1253. Cameron Smith (Queensland)

1254. 141

1255. Queensland Reds

1256. Cameron White

1257. Sir Alex Douglas Home (Middlesex, Oxford University)

1258. Queensland Bulls

1259. Graham Farmer in 1971

1260. Tom Moody, 132

1261. Billy Slater, Melbourne Storm

1262. Edgar Britt

1263. Serena Williams

1264. German, Max Schmeling

1265. 9

1266. Manchester City defeated Stoke City 1-0

1267. Gatewood

1268. NFL Super Bowl championship game

1269. Argentina

1270. Marc Murphy

1271. The Blades

1272. he became the first Tasmanian to play test cricket for Australia

1273. 0

1274. Allen Aylett

1275. Lloyd McDermott against New Zealand in 1962

1276. Barry Foley

1277. Andy Murray

1278. David Furner

1279. Sir Vivian Richards (playing for Antigua 1974)

1280. 1892-93

1281. Glenn Stewart, Manly-Warringah Sea Eagles

1282. Mick Dittman

1283. Justine Henin of Belgium

1284. Canada

1285. 5

1286. Manchester United

1287. Australia

1288. world surfing championship

1289. Thierry Dusautoir

1290. Tony Lockett

1291. Ricky Stuart

1292. Sam Burgess

1293. Mitchell Johnson

1294, Wayne and Max Richardson respectively

1295. Nick Farr-Jones

1296. Pacific

1297. Glenn Archer and Shannon Grant

1298. Cameron Rahles-Rahbula

1299. Gary Player

1300. 1926-27

1301. Ipswich Jets

1302. Roy Higgins

1303. Mary Pierce in 1995 and Monica Seles in 1996

1304. Jack Johnson

1305. 6

1306. 4, (1948-49, 1960-61, 1962-63, 1968-69)

1307. the Western Australian Football League (WAFL)

1308. Coleman Medallist, Fraser Gehrig

1309. 4 ,Australia: Dave Warner (145 & 102), Steve Smith
(162 not out), Michael Clarke (128)
India:V. Kohli (115 & 141)

1310. Peter Thomson

1311. Adelaide 36s

1312. 0 he was runner up three times, 1968, 1973 and 1975

1313. Gary Sobers of the West Indies

1314. Brent Harvey

1315. Michael Lynagh

1316. David Wirrpanda

1317. George Gregan

1318. Angelique Kerber

1319. 1965

1320. 1947-48

1321. Past Brothers, Ipswich and Souths

1322. George Moore

1323. Iva Majoli of Croatia

1324. Australian, Jimmy Carruthers

1325. 10

1326. Queen's Park

1327. American, Matt Kuchar

1328. the Jack Oatey Medal

1329. Australia

1330. Duncan Armstrong

1331. Pakistan

1332. Chinese Fir

1333. Ray Shaw and Tony Shaw respectively

1334. Brad Haddin

1335. the United States

1336. Melbourne Storm and St George Illawarra

1337. Formula One motor racing

1338. Otago Highlanders

1339. 1986

1340. 1977-78

1341. Papua New Guinea

1342. Nash Rawiller

1343. Evonne Goolagong Cawley

1344. Australian, Lionel Rose

1345. 10

1346. Italian, (Carlo Ancelotti and Roberto Mancini)

1347. Daniel Popovic

1348. men's double sculls (rowing)

1349. American golfer, Tiger Woods

1350. Johannesburg South Africa, because it was unsure how black and Asian athletes would be treated or accepted.

1351. racing car driver, Michael Schumacher

1352. Li Na of China

1353. "The Ant"

1354. George Bailey of Australia

1355. two props either side of the hooker

1356. George Piggins Medal

1357. Anthony Rocca

1358. Lankan Rupee

1359. 1 point, round 17 against Geelong in 1899

1360. he designed cricket's Sheffield Shield trophy

1361. Warrington Wolves

1362. Neville Sellwood

1363.   Chris Evert

1364.   Australian, Jeff Fenech

1365.   14

1366.   Liverpool, 2000 and 2006

1367.   8 (1906, 1909, 1913, 1916, 1917, 1919, 1920, 1926)

1368.   West Indies

1369.   awarded to the best South Australian player in an interstate
        Aussie rules match (from 1981)

1370.   Manchester United, Chelsea and Aston Villa

1371.   Wayne Andrews

1372.   Rafael Nadal

1373.   off break

1374.   4 (1985 1986 1991 and 1993)

1375.   the locks

1376.   Steve Ella

1377.   1965-78 Collingwood; 1979 South Melbourne; 1980 Fitzroy

1378.   Essex

1379.   Ben Cousins (West Coast Eagles)

1380.   46

1381.   36

1382.   Harry White

1383.   Venus Williams

1384.   Bob Fitzsimmons of Britain

1385.   7

1386.   Cardiff City in 1927

1387.   2,500 metres

1388.   the Australian Golf Open

1389.   Gary Buckenara

1390.   4 (WBC Super Middleweight; WBA Light-Heavyweight; 2 IBO Cruiser-weight)

1391.   Spanish tennis player Rafael Nadal

1392.   1876

1393.   Swimming

1394.   wheelchair basketball

1395. the hooker

1396. the fairest and best player in a South Australian National Football League grand final

1397. Protectionist

1398. New South Wales

1399. South Melbourne

1400. South Australia

1401. Terry Lamb

1402. Bill Williamson

1403. 2009

1404. James J. Jeffries

1405. 3

1406. Chelsea in 2006-7

1407. Melbourne

1408. Matthew Primus

1409. Australia

1410. Birmingham City

1411. 2001, 2002

1412. Juniper

1413. he became the first Western Australian to play test cricket for Australia

1414. 42 years old

1415. Jonah Lomu

1416. Wild Oats XI

1417. 291

1418. Novak Djokovic

1419. 13 from 6 matches

1420. Greg and Ian Chappell

1421. Michael Cronin

1422. T.J. "Tommy" Smith

1423. 2008

1424. 8

1425. 1 (Mark Ricciuto 2003)

1426. Peter Carey (South Australia v Western Australia at Subiaco in 1981)

1427. 5 (1967, 1968, 1973, 1974 and 1977)

1428. Korean, Jiyai Shin

1429. India

1430. Speedway

1431. Aaron Finch

1432. Trent Bridge, Nottinghamshire England

1433. Hardrada

1434. Oleg Salenko

1435. Rugby Sevens

1436. 1976-77

1437. Swiss tennis player Rodger Federer

1438. Thunderbirds

1439. Royal Navy fleet air arm of the United Kingdom

1440. New South Wales, South Australia and Western Australia

1441. Halifax

1442. T.J. Smith

1443. Lew Hoad

1444. Jess Willard of the U.S. at Toledo Ohio

1445. 9

1446. The Netherlands, South Korea, Australia, Russia and Turkey

1447. Ashlee Mundy

1448. LA Dodgers and the Arizona Diamondbacks

1449. Chris Anderson

1450. Cuba

1451. Adelaide United

1452. Tim Cahill

1453. Headingley

1454. canoeing

1455. 15

1456. Cyclist Phil Anderson

1457. Gary Ablett Senior (Geelong)

1458. sailing

1459. Greg Anderson

1460. Bill Ponsford

1461. Ivan Cleary

1462. Jack Denham

1463. France

1464. Tottenham Hotspur

1465. 11

1466. William J. Millard

1467. Ben Dunk of the Hobart Hurricanes

1468. 11

1469. American, Nathan Adrian

1470. Turkey

1471. Chaz Mostert

1472. King Ingoda

1473. Darren Lockyer

1474. South Africa

1475. Will Carling

1476. Danny Frawley

1477. 1,600 metres

1478. 1923

1479. New Norfolk 1963-68 and Glenorchy 1975-76, 1978-81

1480. Colin Miller, Tasmania 67

1481. Eric Simms

1482. Lee Freedman

1483. Australia

1484. Frenchman, Arsene Wenger

1485. 4

1486. John Eales

1487. South Africa

1488. Bryan Fletcher

1489. India (at Bangalore)

1490. the first rubber core golf ball

1491. Also known as "Yabba" the Sydney Cricket Ground's most
vocal supporter and heckler during the early part of the 20th
century. His statue occupies a spot at the ground in his
honour.

1492. West Coast Eagles

1493. Sydney FC

1494. 10-1

1495. Percy Montgomery

1496. Toronto Raptors

1497. Will Genia

1498. Josep Gombau

1499. Western Sydney Wanderers' Ante Covic

1500. New South Wales

1501. David Brown

1502. Colin Hayes

1503. 2002 v France 3-2

1504. Sir Alex Ferguson

1505. 5

1506. David Andersen

1507. Sam Stosur of Australia

1508. Admire Rakti and Araldo

1509. Sturt

1510. Jordon Spieth

1511. Launceston, Tasmania

1512. Ray Illingworth

1513. Ross Lyon

1514. Cairns Taipans

1515. 4

1516. The Hague in the Netherlands

1517. Adelaide's Daniel Talia

1518. heavyweight

1519. Joeys

1520. 1994-95

1521. 31

1522. David Hayes

1523. Argentina 3-1

1524. Tottenham Hotspur

1525. 5

1526. Stephanie Gilmore

1527. Rodney "Rocket" Eade

1528. Jose Maria Olazabal

1529. Okinawa (Ryukyu)

1530. Australian, Wayne Gardner

1531. Ryan Moore

1532. Ross Glendinning Medal

1533. Lake Placid U.S.A.

1534. Ross Smith

1535. Australia (19-14)

1536. Ricky Ponting, beginning in 2005

1537. Stephen Moore

1538. Ned Gregory of Australia in the first test match in 1877

1539. Cricket; he was a member of the Victorian XI and the Australian aboriginal side that toured England in 1868.

1540. South Australia

1541. Ken Irvine

1542. Gai Waterhouse

1543. Germany

1544. David O'Leary

1545. 0

1546. the Australian PGA Championship tournament

1547. All have scored a century on debut as Australian captain.

1548. Robert Harvey

1549. Judo

1550. Minnesota Vikings

1551. they won the fours championship event at the World Outdoor Bowls championship in Adelaide.

1552. Oscar Wilde

1553. Glen Boss

1554. he had epilepsy

1555. South Africa (defeated Fiji 24-14)

1556. women's New York marathon

1557. 1870

1558. they were all flag bearers for Australia at the opening ceremony of Summer Olympic Games

1559. Johnny Graves

1560. 1950

1561. Frank Burge (1911-1927)

1562. Etienne L.de Mestre

1563. Harvard

1564. they have all been capped 100 times plus for England

1565. 1 (Nat Fyfe 2015)

1566. Lisa Alexander

1567. American golfer Tiger Woods

1568. Black Caviar

1569. Maria Sharapova

1570. John Alexander

1571. Le Chef (ridden by Luke Tarrant)

1572. The Armstrong 500

1573. Poland

1574. Adelaide Lightning

1575. Ballymore in Brisbane

1576. Ted Whitten Senior

1577. Stanislas Wawrinka

1578. Adelaide Strikers

1579. National Women's Soccer League of the United States

1580. South Africa

1581. 4

1582. Rising Fast

1583. John Pius Boland of Great Britain

1584. Bobby Charlton

1585. 1 (Gary Ablett 2013)

1586. Melbourne Cricket Ground, Melbourne Australia

1587. 5

1588. Dear Demi

1589. Eric MacKensie

1590. Atlanta Falcons

1591. Southern Suns

1592. Michael Clarke (259 n.o.) Mike Hussey (100) and Ed Cowan (136) for Australia and Jacques Kallis (147) and Hashim Amla (104) for South Africa.

1593. Melbourne United

1594. Muggsy Bogues (5' 3" or 160cm,Washington Bullets, Charlotte Hornets, Warriors and Toronto Raptors)

1595. England (defeated Samoa 29-21)

1596. Oxford-Cambridge rowing race

1597. Wales

1598. Ray French (East Fremantle)

1599. Steven Smith

1600. Graham McKenzie

1601. he had arm injuries

1602. 3

1603. Charlotte Cooper of Great Britain

1604. Fitzroy

1605. Gordon Banks

1606. James Graham

1607. 1839

1608. Hobart Hurricanes

1609. 1897

1610. Eric Simms

1611. Australian Ricky Ponting (versus Pakistan)

1612. Nathan Burke

1613. Michelle Wie

1614. Firethorn

1615. The Singapore Slingers

1616. Mark Twain

1617. six

1618. Wagga Wagga NSW

1619. Wembley Stadium in London

1620. Ian Redpath and Gary Cosier

1621. Eddie Lamsden

1622. they are among the horses which have won the W.S. Cox
       Plate twice

1623. gold- Atlanta, silver-Sydney

1624. Fitzroy

1625. Gary Lineker

1626. Chris Goulding

1627. Tasmanian, Andrew Robinson

1628. McLaren

1629. Mrs H.B. Bonney in 1932

1630. New Zealand Breakers

1631. Baltimore

1632. an ancient unit of measurement (600 feet) which was the
       length of the ancient Olympic   event of the same name
       used in the original Olympic Games. From the "stade"
       came the word "stadium" a place where the event was held.

1633. Copra America

1634. Pakistan

1635. The Adelaide City Eagles

1636. White Nose

1637. Oliver Goss

1638. Cheltenham

1639. Wrest Point Tassie Van Demons

1640. Richard Hadlee of New Zealand

1641. the Ron Coote Cup

1642. they are horses which have won the Melbourne Cup/Cox Plate double

1643. 1963

1644. American, Joe Louis

1645. Kevin Murray

1646. Allan Ball Junior.

1647. Brandy

1648. he took part in an unofficial Australian tour of South Africa in 1985-86 and 1986-87

1649. Mitchell Johnson of Australia

1650. Sebastian Vettel (Formula One)

1651. 87 (13 from a century)

1652. South Adelaide

1653. Australian women's soccer

1654. Brett Maher

1655. 1999-2000

1656. Real Love ridden by William Pike

1657. Ian Synman

1658. West Coast Eagles fairest and best award

1659. Serena Williams

1660. 1983

1661. John Raper

1662. 1922

1663. Czech Republic

1664. Fremantle Dockers

1665. Kevin Keegan

1666. Adam Cooney (2008) Western Bulldogs

1667. Southern Hotshots

1668. Don Langsford and Ross Glendinning

1669. Norwood

1670. the American League and the National League

1671. 42

1672. Scotland (2004)

1673. Carolina Panthers

1674. Brett Aitken

1675. 2007-2008

1676. Western Sydney Wanderers

1677. Jamaican

1678. The Vipers

1679. Peter Pan

1680. Craig McDermott

1681. John O'Neill

1682. 18

1683. U.S.

1684. Essendon's John Coleman

1685. Alan Shearer

1686. Olga Korbut

1687. Colin Cowdrey in a test against Australia at Edgbaston 1968.

1688. Australian, Casey Stoner

1689. South Korea

1690. show jumping (its a type of jump with two rails set even or unevenly apart in various distance combinations

1691. Dawn Fraser of Australia

1692. West Coast Waves

1693. Black Sea

1694. 10

1695. Melbourne Tigers

1696. completed the first mainland to Rottnest swim

1697. 1992

1698. 7.26 kg or 16.01 lbs

1699. Ezzard Charles, title holder (1950) and Rocky Marciano, contender (1951)

1700. Ricky Ponting

1701. Ray Price

1702. Harold Badger

1703. Australia

1704. 6 times (1926-1930 and 1933)

1705. Paul Gascoigne

1706. Aaron Finch

1707. Lacrosse

1708. cycling

1709. (Athletics) Walking, Commonwealth Games gold medallist

1710. 1975

1711. Chinese Grand Prix

1712. Sydney journalist, Tony Horstead

1713. they have all made double centuries on test debut

1714. Graham Arnold

1715. New Zealand Breakers

1716. Mandurah, Western Australia

1717. Dean Cox

1718. 48

1719. he became the first player of any country to score a test century in both innings of a test match.

1720. West Indian, Malcolm Marshall

1721. 2

1722. Dulcify

1723. U.S and Australia, U.S winning 2-1

1724. Dick Lee

1725. Sir Stanley Matthews

1726. Madi Robinson

1727. Brazilian

1728. Dawn Fraser

1729. 12   5 for 134 and 7 for 152

1730. Brisbane Roar

1731. Lancashire County Cricket Club, Manchester England

1732. Johnny Weissmuller in 1912

1733. Prince of Penzance

1734. Brian Lara in April 2004 versus England (400 not out)

1735. Westate Wildcats

1736. she was the first woman to swim from the mainland to Rottnest Island in Western Australia

1737. Tasmania

1738. David Rudisha

1739. Jason Day

1740. Steve Waugh

1741. Bernie Purcell

1742. Peter Cook

1743. 1989

1744. Ezzard Charles (winner) and Jersey Joe Walcott

1745. 146

1746. PGA Championship

1747. South Sydney

1748. Germany, 18

1749. Mark Schwarzer

1750. New Orleans (Saints) in the state of Louisiana.

1751. Alex Gibb

1752. 89 matches

1753. because of New Zealand's sporting contacts with South Africa

1754. San Francisco Giants

1755. West Sydney Westars and Sydney Supersonics

1756. Andrew McLeod

1757. the first golf club in America, the St Andrews Golf Club

1758. 1986

1759. he was the first to clear 7 feet in the high jump

1760. Denis Lillee

1761. 1966

1762. Billy Cook

1763. Australia

1764. 4 times (1987, 1991 St Kilda), (1996,1998 Sydney)

1765. Jack Charlton

1766. they were charged with bribery

1767. Phillip Island, Victoria

1768. Tommie Smith, USA ,in 1968 at the Mexico Olympics (19.83 sec)

1769. the butterfly swimming stroke

1770. Marjorie Jackson (Helsinki 1952) and Betty Cuthbert (Melbourne 1956)

1771. Peter Bell

1772. Rafael Nadal

1773. goal umpire, Alexander Salton killed at the Battle of Fromelles in France in 1916

1774. Chicago

1775. Townsville Suns

1776. Australian Open men's softball championship

1777. Chris Froome

1778. Jeff Kennett

1779. Brian Peake

1780. Justin Langer

1781. Dick Dunn

1782. Billy Cook

1783. Czech Republic

1784. Garry Ablett Senior of Geelong

1785. 26

1786. motorcycle speedway

1787. Calgary, Canada

1788. Gold Coast Australia

1789. he was the first, first grade cricketer to be suspended by the Victorian Cricket Association for striking an opponent during a match.

1790. Sachin Tendulkar

1791. Geelong

1792. Johnathan Thurston (Queensland)

1793. Geelong

1794. 23

1795. Illawarra Hawks

1796. 5

1797. Royal Australian Air Force

1798. Paula Radcliffe

1799. Italy, Uruguay and Costa-Rica

1800. Steve Waugh

1801. Johnny King

1802. Mollison

1803. Dusseldorf, Germany

1804. University

1805. 4

1806. Craig Williams

1807. Peter Schwab

1808. Gary Player of South Africa and Jack Nicklaus of the U.S.

1809. Somalia

1810. Jane Saville of Australia

1811. Morocco

1812. Hull City

1813. Montreal 1976

1814. East Perth

1815. The Tall Blacks

1816. Australian Open Women's Softball Championship

1817. Dennis Cometti

1818. 1945

1819. Oslo, Norway

1820. Mike Hussey

1821. Five-eighths

1822. So You Think

1823.   Novak Djokovic

1824.   Fred Fanning

1825.   Daniel Passarela

1826.   Southern Steel's Jhaniele Fowler

1827.   Peter Daicos

1828.   the Showdown Medal

1829.   New York Yankees

1830.   Florida

1831.   Newtown

1832.   Kew Jaliens

1833.   because of England's attitude to sporting contacts with South
         Africa

1834.   Rory McIlvoy, Northern Ireland and Lee Westwood ,England

1835.   4, 1988 (Seoul) , 1992 (Barcelona), 1996 (Atlanta) and 2000
         (Sydney)

1836.   Dublin in Ireland

1837.   Australia

1838.	Kim Hughes

1839.	4kg or 8.8 lbs

1840.	Shane Warne

1841.	Harry Bath

1842.	Brent Thomson

1843.	Petra Kvitova

1844.	Michael Tuck

1845.	Argentina

1846.	5

1847.	Andrew Vlahov

1848.	Pampas

1849.	Rocky Marciano

1850.	6

1851.	first person to have ever clear 8 feet in high jump

1852.	Sav Rocca

1853.	Carl Lewis (Jim Hines 1968 was at altitude and Bob Hayes, 1963 was wind assisted)

1854. Cristiano Ronaldo

1855. Phil Smyth

1856. Bendigo Spirit

1857. Brendon McCullum 2nd test verses India, February 2014.

1858. James Rodriguez (Columbia)

1859. St Kilda

1860. South African Dale Steyn

1861. Because of his high punting of the football which was referred to as a bomb

1862. W.S. Cox Plate

1863. Pete Sampras of the U.S.

1864. Delicacy

1865. Turin

1866. Darren Beadman

1867. Jack Dyer

1868. an annual award given since 1998 to an Australian sports performance which recognises sporting achievement which has inspired Australians.

1869. Paul Wade

1870. a women's golf tournament played between teams from the U.S. and Europe

1871. 400m and the 800m

1872. men's softball

1873. Usman Khawaja

1874. John Greening

1875. 12th

1876. Old Trafford cricket ground Manchester, England

1877. Fiji

1878. 2,200 metres

1879. Tom Hafey

1880. West Indian Leslie Hylton

1881. 1948

1882. Fields of Omagh

1883. Roger Federer

1884. Michael Dokes

1885.	43 years and 48 days

1886.	Barcelona

1887.	Haarlem in the Netherlands

1888.	Arizona Cardinals

1889.	Haydn Bunton Junior

1890.	Nathan Lyon

1891.	Andy Green of Britain

1892.	Lucas Neill

1893.	Fremantle, Western Australia

1894.	Japan

1895.	The Minnesota Timberwolves

1896.	Peter Wilson

1897.	Southern Cross

1898.	Sydney, Australia

1899.	Alex Brosque

1900.	Englishman Ian Botham (1986)

1901. Jack Gibson

1902. Maree Lyndon on Argonaut Style in 1987

1903. Bob and Mike Bryan

1904. Richmond, Collingwood ,Geelong and Sydney

1905. 2004

1906. Lance Armstrong

1907. South Australian Football Association

1908. Philipp Lahm

1909. New Jersey Devils, New York Islanders and the New York Rangers

1910. George Bailey

1911. Robert De Castella

1912. pole vaulter Steve Hooker

1913. New Zealand

1914. Michael Tuck

1915. Minnesota Timberwolves and the San Antonio Spurs

1916. Magnolia

1917.   2007

1918.   Jason Dufner

1919.   4th and 11th respectively

1920.   Phil Tufnel

1921.   Ted Goodwin (St George) and Ed Sulkowicz (Parramatta)

1922.   1925 (ABC)

1923.   Lindsay Davenport

1924.   Jock McHale

1925.   Sydney FC

1926.   1979

1927.   Mike Ellis

1928.   Les Fong

1929.   the Australian Golf Open

1930.   Australian, Kathy Watt

1931.   1901

1932.   Queensland Bulls

1933. New Zealand born, Otto Cribb who died after a welter-weight title fight in July 1901.

1934. St George Dragons

1935. Ricky Grace

1936. South Australia defeated New South Wales by 57 runs

1937. Collingwood

1938. Shaun Marsh (148), Steve Smith (100) and Dave Warner (115)

1939. Dowerin

1940. Geoff Boycott

1941. Steve Edge

1942. Peter St Aubans eight days short of his thirteenth birthday. (riding Briseis in 1876)

1943. Lisa Raymond (U.S.) and Sam Stosur (Australia)

1944. Mike Tyson

1945. 9

1946. Adelaide United, Perth Glory and the Newcastle Jets

1947. 1979

1948.	Rene Kink

1949.	Cameron White

1950.	Faster, Higher, Stronger

1951.	Jeremy Hayward

1952.	Muhammad Ali

1953.	Mel Whinnen

1954.	1902

1955.	Lindsay Gaze

1956.	Collingwood at the MCG

1957.	South African, Gary Player

1958.	Shooting (7 gold, 8 silver and 2 bronze)

1959.	Francois Pienaar

1960.	Jack Hobbs in 1929

1961.	Des Morris

1962.	Sheila Laxon in 2001

1963.	Jonas Bjorkman of Sweden

1964. Coach- Norm Smith and Captain-Ron Barassi

1965. Central Coast Mariners

1966. Tom Stingsby

1967. yellow and green diagonal stripes with white cap

1968. the Philadelphia Flyers

1969. Lionel Messi

1970. American basketball player, Michael Jordan

1971. "Best Goal"

1972. he broke the world water speed record, setting a speed of 511.13 kmph in a vehicle named "The Spirit of Australia"

1973. Australia 34, New Zealand 2

1974. tennis player Novak Djokovic

1975. 5

1976. Li Na of China

1977. 2000 and 2001

1978. Mac, a black Scots terrier

1979. Denver Broncos

1980.   Ricky Ponting of Australia

1981.   Wales

1982.   AJC Sire Produce Stakes

1983.   Martina Navratilova

1984.   after Melbourne's premiership in 1964, beginning with Carlton in 1965

1985.   Sydney FC

1986.   Nathan Sharpe

1987.   Lake Karrinyup Country Club in Perth Western Australia

1988.   the Lansdowne Cup

1989.   Lance Franklin

1990.   Rose Bay

1991.   Squaw Valley, U.S.A.

1992.   Australian, Kieren Perkins

1993.   Phil Tierney

1994.   Western Bulldogs (Footscray)

1995.   the Australian women's basketball team

1996.   Barry Hall

1997.   Germany

1998.   Port Adelaide Magpies (SANFL)

1999.   Melissa Breen

2000.   Wasim Akram

2001.   England

2002.   Yalumba Stakes

2003.   7 :(1987, 1988, 1989, 1990, 1993, 1995, 1996)

2004.   Ron Barassi

2005.   Melbourne Victory

2006.   Hawthorn 1982-92, Sydney 1994 and Collingwood 1995

2007.   Atlantic, Metropolitan, (Eastern conference) Pacific, Central
        (Western Conference)

2008.   Perth Heat

2009.   1887, won by Nimrod

2010.   Buster Douglas

2011.   Brumbies

2012. Emile Heskey

2013. Sebastian Vettel

2014. South Africa

2015. Seattle Storm

2016. 1975

2017. 18

2018. Inverness Caledonian Thistle F.C.

2019. West Coast's Matt Priddis

2020. Terry Alderman, Australia, 1981 and 1989 Australia verses England

2021. France

2022. Futurity Stakes

2023. 2, 2001 and 2002

2024. Melbourne

2025. Central Coast Mariners

2026. James Hardy

2027. David Ferrer

2028. Roselee Jencke of the Queensland Firebirds

2029. Victorian Spirit

2030. Pittsburgh Penguins

2031. Andrew Collins

2032. James Hopes

2033. 100 metre hurdles

2034. Manuel Neuer (Germany)

2035. 1981

2036. Jack Sheedy

2037. Canberra Capitals

2038. Nathan Berry

2039. David Warner

2040. 153

2041. 1988

2042. the Goodwood, previously known as the Goodwood Handicap

2043. 1992

2044. Neil Balme

2045. 36

2046. Sonar

2047. American basketball player Michael Jordan

2048. Kansas City Chiefs and the St Louis Rams

2049. Manly Warringah Sea Eagles

2050. the New York Highlanders

2051. Joachim Low

2052. 312

2053. 1972

2054. Woodville

2055. 5   (1994, 1995, 1996, 1998, 2008)

2056. November 1960

2057. Brisbane Bullets and Geelong Supercats

2058. 243

2059. a biennial world amateur golf championship for women

2060. they all played for both Pakistan and India

2061. Fiji

2062. the Lightning Stakes

2063. 2003

2064. Neale Daniher

2065. 2009-2010

2066. 21

2067. 2kg

2068. world heavyweight champion Vladimir Klitchko

2069. Australia

2070. Boston Bruins

2071. Hibernians

2072. Merrett-Murray Medal (named after Rodger Merrett and Kevin Murray)

2073. the fairest and best Western Australian player in an AFL State of Origin game awarded in 1995 and 1998.

2074. West Coast Fever

2075. 1998/99

2076. a gold watch

2077. American golfer Tiger Woods

2078. diving

2079. South African Ernie Els

2080. he became the youngest test cricketer at 14 years and 227 days when debut against Zimbabwe.

2081. 1996

2082. Australia, England, Japan, Singapore, Hong Kong and Dubai

2083. Novak Djokovic

2084. Garry Lyon

2085. 2010-2011

2086. Craig Fitzgibbon (New South Wales)

2087. New South Wales

2088. Michael Clarke

2089. North Melbourne

2090. Jim Cassidy

2091.   Andrew Durante

2092.   7th   1998

2093.   George Smith

2094.   American golfer Tiger Woods

2095.   2007/2008

2096.   Evander Holyfield

2097.   Queensland

2098.   Australian, Casey Stoner

2099.   Novak Djokovic

2100.   the United States and Canada in 1844

2101.   New Zealand (trophy), Fiji (plate), Tonga (bowl)

2102.   Chatham

2103.   Venus Williams

2104.   Carlton, 1906, 1907 and 1908

2105.   New Zealand Knights

2106.   Geoff Marsh

2107   he became the first black American to play Major League
        baseball in the modern era.

2108.   25

2109.   16

2110.   Seattle

2111.   St George Dragons (1993-96 and 1998) Brisbane Broncos
        (1997) St George Illawarra (1999-2000)

2112.   Mark Mickan

2113.   Brentford, Chelsea, Queens Park Rangers and Fulham

2114.   7:   2002-2008

2115.   Bullen Boomers

2116.   Perth Wildcats

2117.   Ashley Sampi

2118.   Bobby Skilton of South Melbourne

2119.   27 years

2120.   1846

2121.   4

2122. Agua Caliente Handicap in Tijuana Mexico in 1932

2123. Henry Austin

2124. John Nicholls

2125. North Queensland Fury

2126. Brazilian club, Corinthians

2127. the Maroons

2128. Curling

2129. Victoire

2130. Alex Jesaulenko

2131. a Fijian war dance performed by the Fijian national team before their rugby union matches

2132. 17

2133. the Buffalo Sabres

2134. Charles Bannerman

2135. Canberra Capitals

2136. Andy Murray

2137 South Sydney Rabbitohs

2138. the Great North Run

2139. Arsenal

2140. an Australian aboriginal team

2141. 8

2142. Timaru

2143. cricket club

2144. 25

2145. Bernd Stange

2146. the Alex Jesaulenko Medal

2147. 1993 Ashes series

2148. They were 100 to 1 winners of the Cup

2149. Trevor Bayliss

2150. Sebastian Vettel

2151. Mitchell Johnson of Australia

2152. Queensland (Townsville)

2153. Simon Gerrans

2154. Red Cadeaux 2014, 2013 and 2011

2155. Dandenong Rangers

2156. Israel Folau

2157. Northamptonshire (2001-2003), Gloucestershire (2004) , Durham (2005)

2158. Australia, Wales, England, New Zealand, Scotland and Canada

2159. Gabriel Medina

2160. "The Demon Bowler"

2161. 4

2162. Night Raid

2163. Ivo Karlovic of Croatia

2164. 6 times

2165. David Parkin

2166. 1977

2167. Nambour in Queensland

2168. Kings XI Punjab

2169.   Richmond

2170.   Blue

2171.   West Ham United

2172.   1981

2173.   David Warner (124) and Michael Clarke (113)

2174.   a high jumping competition in the equestrian sport of show jumping

2175.   Women's National Basketball League

2176.   Ian Healy

2177.   Michael Thwaite

2178.   1880

2179.   Brazil

2180.   Billy Murdoch

2181.   21

2182.   Randwick Guineas

2183.   the match took 11 hours and 5 minutes to complete

2184.   Stephen Kernahan

2185. Perth Glory

2186. Neil Balme

2187. Leeds United, Liverpool and Galatasaray in Turkey

2188. Australia versus France

2189. Ochre

2190. 9 gold and 3 silver

2191. Darren Lockyer

2192. St Moritz, Switzerland

2193. 2003

2194. Reading F.C.

2195. Women's National Basketball League

2196. the Perth Scorcher's Craig Simmons

2197. the Commonwealth Golf Club

2198. Goldie the Kiwi bird

2199. Ford's Mark Winterbottom

2200. Clem Hill

2201. 18 years and 83 days

2202. Vic Rail

2203. "Little Miss Poker Face"

2204. Denis Pagan

2205. Franz Beckenbauer

2206. 46

2207. she became the first female owner of a winning Melbourne Cup horse when Patrobas won the event.

2208. Joe DiMaggio

2209. Zarina Diyas of Kazakhstan

2210. the Montreal Canadiens

2211. Bayern Munich

2212. Sir Michael Fay

2213. 8 year old gelding

2214. Redbud

2215. Women's National Basketball League

2216. Ricky Grace

2217. Jim Richards

2218. Marcus North

2219. France

2220. Cootamundra

2221. 16

2222. Cyril Small

2223. 16

2224. Craig Bradley

2225. Real Madrid

2226. 1907

2227. Justin Langer

2228. squash

2229. 29

2230. Germany

2231. Luke Darcy

2232. featherweight

2233. Michael Kasprowicz

2234. Ken McAullay (East Perth)

2235. Perth Breakers and Perth Lynx

2236. Liz Ellis

2237. 7 for 40

2238. the biennial Eisenhower Trophy for amateur men golfers

2239. Jersey Joe Walcott

2240. 117

2241. 5

2242. Comic Court

2243. Newport Rhode Island

2244. 1970, Carlton versus Collingwood

2245. Bayern Munich

2246. 1998

2247. Lucas Neill

2248. 8th-1987

2249. Hugh Bowman

2250. Sheffield United

2251. they became the first women to be awarded the Royal Life
Saving Society Award of Merit and the Silver Medallion.

2252. Tasmanian Devils

2253. Australia

2254. 2004

2255. Phoenix Mercury

2256. 2003

2257. Black Tycoon

2258. South Sydney Rabbitoh's Sam Burgess

2259. Cyclist Anna Meares

2260. Douglas Jardine

2261. 52   (5 tries and 16 goals)

2262. J.J. (Johnny) Miller

2263. 37

2264. they were all in the losing sides on the day

2265.   Internazionale (Inter Milan)

2266.   Sri Lanka

2267.   Leighton Aspell

2268.   Phil Hughes versus Sri Lanka MCG January 2013

2269.   buffering

2270.   12

2271.   American Major League baseball winner of the World Series.

2272.   Diana Prazak

2273.   the Ottawa Senators

2274.   the United States

2275.   Perth Wildcats, Canberra Cannons and the Geelong Supercats

2276.   Leigh Matthews

2277.   winners of the women's 4 x100 freestyle relay and a new
        world record, achieved at the 2014 Commonwealth Games
        in Glasgow Scotland.

2278.   Brisbane Heat

2279.   Australian, Johnny Famechon

2280. Australian wicket keeper Bert Oldfield

2281. 24

2282. Todman

2283. 4

2284. Lenny Hayes St Kilda and Scott Pendlebury Collingwood

2285. Adelaide, South Australia

2286. Les Scheinflug against North Korea in 1965

2287. cruiser-weight or junior heavyweight

2288. Perth Cup Day (New Years Day)

2289. Leeds

2290. Anna Meares (track cycling)

2291. heptathlon and long jump

2292. Jeff Fenech (2002) and Kostya Tszyu (2011)

2293. Seven

2294. Australia and Brazil

2295. Brisbane Bullets and the West Adelaide Bearcats

2296. the natural arc a horse's body takes as it jumps over an obstacle

2297. Southern Steel

2298. 403

2299. Spaniard Marc Marquez

2300. 1934 between Australia and England in Brisbane

2301. 27

2302. 29

2303. John Newcombe and Tony Roche

2304. Joseph Louis Barrow

2305. South Fremantle

2306. Rale Rasic

2307. a variation of association football (soccer) which is played on a smaller pitch usually   indoors

2308. Ernie Merrick

2309. Peter Senior

2310. Yellow Jasmine

2311. Misha or Mishka the Russian bear

2312. Australian Michael Clarke

2313. Nandina

2314. 2000

2315. Brisbane Bullets

2316. Lewis Hamilton

2317. 5: 2000, 2002 to 2005

2318. Peter Bell

2319. Jeremy Paul

2320. "Nugget"

2321. 69

2322. 19

2323. Martina Navratilova and Pam Shriver

2324. Les Darcy

2325. The Lake Oval

2326. Terry Venables

2327. 5

2328. American golfer Tiger Woods

2329. the men's marathon

2330. Sheffield Wednesday

2331. Hungarian

2332. Chicago Blackhawks

2333. Brazil

2334. Honda

2335. North Melbourne Giants

2336. Casey Stoner

2337. team equestrian show jumping

2338. Graham Moss

2339. Marcos Flores (Adelaide United)

2340. St Kilda

2341. 12

2342. Eurythmic

2343. 32 minutes 6-0 6-0

2344.   "The Blood Bath"

2345.   31-0

2346.   Rafael Nadal

2347.   South African Air Force

2348.   Jason Gillespie (verses Bangladesh)

2349.   2009

2350.   the Toronto Maples Leafs

2351.   "Be Active Tour"

2352.   110

2353.   Fitzroy and Essendon

2354.   Alex Leapai

2355.   Alan Black

2356.   David Mueller

2357.   8

2358.   Wild Oats XI

2359.   Jim Cassidy

2360. the West Indies

2361. 161

2362. Better Loosen Up

2363. Spencer Gore

2364. James J. Braddock

2365. Sydney Swans, verses West Coast (201) and Essendon (239) in 1987

2366. John Aloisi

2367. aerial skiing

2368. Peter Pan

2369. Germany

2370. Wayne Gardiner of Australia

2371. Bradford Bulls

2372. Michel Bourez

2373. Hyderabad

2374. Troy Wilson

2375. Mike Ellis

2376. Missy Franklin (Swimming)

2377. luge

2378. John Hampshire

2379. Brett Prebble

2380. Pakistan

2381. France

2382. Carbine

2383. 1884

2384. Anthony Mundine

2385. 1996, losing to North Melbourne

2386. Su-Hyun Oh of Australia

2387. Micky Mantle

2388. Kevin Sheedy

2389. 29

2390. he became the first person to score a test century at Lord's cricket ground in London (versus Australia)

2391. Women members were allowed for the first time

2392. W.A. Diamonds

2393. canoeing

2394. Chris Ciriello

2395. Adrian Hurley

2396. Chris Latham

2397. American golfer Tiger Woods

2398. the first rugby union match between the two colonies

2399. Matthew and Steven Febey of Melbourne F.C.

2400. Englishman, Jim Laker

2401. the Penguins

2402. Chatham

2403. 15 years and 285 days

2404. Rick Quade

2405. Fabio Grosso

2406. Carbine

2407. 7

2408. Lote Tugiri

2409. John Kennedy

2410. Carolina Hurricanes

2411. Michael Doohan of Australia

2412. Australia and England

2413. winner of the Stawell Easter Gift

2414. his coach Sean Foley

2415. Trevor Gleeson

2416. Max Baer

2417. Mark Ella

2418. Gary Sidebottom

2419. he head-butted Paris St Germain midfielder Thiago Motta

2420. Australian Matthew Hayden (375)

2421. Canada

2422. Grand Flaneur

2423. Althea Gibson of the U.S. 1956 French Championship

2424. Paul Kelly

2425. Zinedine Zidane

2426. Norm Goss Medal

2427. Gold Coast, Queensland Australia

2428. Bill Howard

2429. Sheffield Wednesday

2430. BMX

2431. IndyCar series motor racing

2432. Klee Wyck the Orca killer whale

2433. tennis player Roger Federer

2434. Williams F1

2435. Brendan Joyce

2436. Metropolitan Division

2437. a delivery that has not had any runs scored off it

2438. Mark Viduka

2439. Frank Worrell

2440. 1928

2441. Lions

2442. Bletchingly

2443. Maud Watson in 1884

2444. Australian/Russian Kostya Tszyu

2445. Tony Lockett of Sydney

2446. Manchester City and Arsenal

2447. Queensland

2448. 8

2449. TP52 Balance

2450. Bethanie Mattek-Sands (U.S.) and Lucie Safarova (Czech Republic)

2451. Atlantic

2452. Canberra Cavalry

2453. Kevin "Cowboy" Neale

2454. Flowering Crab Apple

2455. Brian Goorjian

2456. Honda

2457. Tassie Tigers

2458. Ducati

2459. Alastair Clackson

2460. 1932

2461. Huddersfield

2462. Malcolm Johnston

2463. approximately 2oz

2464. St Kilda

2465. The Netherlands

2466. New York Mets and the San Francisco Giants

2467. Nathan Sharpe

2468. the flipper

2469. Sri Lanka

2470. Scott Chipperfield

2471. he was the first Australian player to bat through an innings

2472. 3   (1984 1995 and 2006)

2473. Luke Hodge

2474. Sapporo, Japan

2475. St Kilda defeated Canberra Cannons 94-93

2476. Cheju Island South Korea in 1976

2477. Rafael Nadal

2478. Samuel Beckett who played for Dublin University during the 1925 and 1926 season. He won the Nobel Prize for Literature in 1969.

2479. Florida Panthers

2480. 1930

2481. The Bati

2482. Bill Collins

2483. 1897

2484. Paul Roos

2485. AFC Ajax and A.C. Milan

2486. Leicester City

2487. light heavyweight

2488. Blackpool F.C.

2489. a small horse jump usually consisting of a wooden rails about three metres apart supported off the ground by x stands at each end.

2490. the Futsalroos

2491. Nikolai Topor-Stanley

2492. Primo Carnera

2493. Frans Thijssen

2494. a Tongan war dance performed by the Tongan national team before a rugby union match

2495. Boston Celtics

2496. Wotan

2497. Ducati

2498. Bryron Pickett (premiership; North Melbourne 1999
Port Adelaide 2004

2499. Rafael Nadal

2500. 1952

Abbreviations

AFL	Australian Football League
AJC	Australian Jockey Club
APS	Association of Professional Surfers
FA	Football Association
FC	Football Club
FIFA	Federation Internationale de Football Federation
FINA	Federation Internationale de Natation (International Swimming Federation)
IBF	International Boxing Federation
IBO	International Boxing Organisation
LPGA	Ladies Professional Golfers Association
MCG	Melbourne Cricket Ground
NAB	National Australia Bank
NBA	National Basketball Association
NBL	National Basketball League
NFL	National Football League
NHL	National Hockey League
NRL	National Rugby League
NSMRL	New South Wales Rugby League
PGA	Professional Golfers Association
QRL	Queensland Rugby League
SANFL	South Australian National Football League
UEFA	Union of European Football Associations
VFA	Victorian Football Association
VFL	Victorian Football League
WACA	Western Australian Cricket Association
WAFL	Western Australian Football League
WANFL	Western Australian National Football League
WBC	World Boxing Council
WBO	World Boxing Organisation

Lightning Source UK Ltd.
Milton Keynes UK
UKHW010802110619
344201UK00007B/130/P